W9-BYV-316

LIFE'S MESSY,
LIVE HAPPY

ALSO BY CY WAKEMAN

No Ego

The Reality-Based Rules of the Workplace

Reality-Based Leadership

LIFE'S MESSY, LIVE HAPPY

Things Don't Have to Be Perfect for You to Be Content

CY WAKEMAN

ST. MARTIN'S PRESS

NEW YORK

First published in the United States by St. Martin's Press,
an imprint of St. Martin's Publishing Group

www.stmartins.com

Designed by Meighan Cavanaugh

Library of Congress Cataloging-in-Publication Data

Names: Wakeman, Cy, author.
Title: Life's messy, live happy : things don't have to be perfect for you
    to be content / Cy Wakeman.
Description: First edition. | New York : St. Martin's Press, [2022]
Identifiers: LCCN 2021047615 | ISBN 9781250275165 (hardcover) |
    ISBN 9781250275172 (ebook)
Subjects: LCSH: Happiness. | Contentment. | Attitude (Psychology)
Classification: LCC BF575.H27 W347 2022 | DDC 158—dc23/
    eng/20211006
LC record available at https://lccn.loc.gov/2021047615

Our books may be purchased in bulk for promotional, educational, or business
use. Please contact your local bookseller or the Macmillan Corporate and
Premium Sales Department at 1-800-221-7945, extension 5442, or
by email at MacmillanSpecialMarkets@macmillan.com.

First Edition: 2022

10 9 8 7 6 5 4 3 2 1

*For the women whose strength and love
changed my DNA and my Destiny.
And to Cathy, whose name is
written on my heart.*

CONTENTS

AT THE WATER

Here I am, back at the water.

The water is what calls to me when it is time to gather courage, make a life pivot, wash away some kind of devastation, and begin again. I have said goodbye at the water's edge to people I love, to people who are dead or who are dead to me. I have almost lost my life in the water, only to return to the surface for more. I have soaked in the water as baptism, emerging with wisdom.

This time, I'm watching the restless Pacific Ocean crash onto the shore from a second-floor balcony in Mexico. The waves are dramatic, gathering and expending a force that creates undulating fountains of foamy spray. Depending on the time of day or what is happening with the sky, the water's color changes minute by minute, from deep indigo, to azure, to pale aqua.

I'm exhausted.

I've come back to the water because, once again, my life is messy.

As I look out at the beautiful, churning ocean, my heartbeat runs wild, like I'm on the bottom drop of a roller coaster. My stomach is jumping like it does on that Silly Silo ride where everything spins, faster and faster. The floor drops away and you're pinned to the side, unable to move. I had such high hopes for myself, that I would walk through the world enlightened, perfect, acing the Test of Life.

In the cool morning shadows, I stand on the balcony doubting myself, worrying about the future and wondering about the choices I am making. I feel misunderstood. In the last week, I've watched three months of business engagements, my livelihood, disappear in the face of a pandemic. My best friend just got a PET scan back, cancer has taken up residence in her liver, and she will be entering hospice. And I'm feeling completely betrayed. I've learned that my husband, from whom I'm separated but not divorced, has taken up with his high school sweetheart and others, violating our informal agreement not to date as we try to negotiate our future. He's even admitted to having trysts in our Mexican home. I want to resist the suck of a downward spiral, but my ego keeps seducing me with stories.

My head is dizzy from all the questions spinning in the center of the Silly Silo ride: How can I be so successful in one area of my life and unsuccessful in another? What if I can't rebuild my business? How can I see myself so differently from the way my husband now describes me? What kind of fun house mirror has distorted my self-image? What if the accusations I'm hearing— that I am materialistic, full of ego, and undesirable—are real? What if I'm nothing without him? My dearest friend is dying, and how will I live in a world without her? How can I ever learn to live with the gaping holes left behind? I've spent so much of my life helping others, but what if nobody is there for me? What if I can only be loved for what I give, and never for who I am? What if I've peaked? What if I'm a failure?

What if I lose everything and end up all alone?

My mind knows these Silly Silo feelings will pass, but in this moment, they're unpleasant and painful. I share some of this with a friend sitting on the balcony beside me.

"It doesn't surprise me you're feeling this way right now," she says. "But sometime, you should let me tell you a story about a girl I know. Her life was so messed up that she lived for several months in a pup tent by the lake because she had nowhere else to go. She was resilient, and she came out just fine."

Oh yeah. That girl.

That was the first time my messy life drove me to the water.

I was twenty-one years old, and my bad choices had put me into a serious, dangerous predicament. I'd been dating Joe (not his real name) since I was nineteen. We worked together at an incredible restaurant. He was an adorable, handsome, funny soccer star. He was charming, brilliant, and well-read—popular in a way I never had been. When he chose me, I was beyond thrilled. I honestly couldn't believe he wanted to be with *me*. But he did, so I broke off my engagement to a young man who was dear to me, had been good to me. I set him aside to satisfy the craving to be part of Joe's glittering in-crowd.

It didn't take long to discover the high price required to be loved by Joe. Sacrifices had to be made. We both worked really hard, going to school full-time and waiting tables at night. After work, there were parties with lots of alcohol and drugs. To keep being chosen, I had to be vigilant: always looking good, saying the right things, and doing what he wanted me to do. To be part of his world meant partying, drinking a lot, using cocaine—and not infrequently.

During the day, at school, I was the consummate good girl, earning straight A's, knowing the answers, being the professors' golden student. At night, I poured whatever was left of my energy, boosted by the drugs, into being loved by Joe.

Soon the fun started to feel pretty empty, and then scary. I discovered that, even though I was the girlfriend Joe presented to the world, he wasn't faithful to me. He wasn't choosing me exclusively. One day, I found him in bed with my best girlfriend. It should have enraged me. I should have left immediately. Instead, it negated me.

I questioned my choices and attempted to leave. But each time I tried, he became more controlling, demeaning, and belittling. His language sounded familiar. He repeated unjust tropes from my childhood, and demanded that I keep the peace. He told me I was the flawed one and created an obstacle course of things I needed to accomplish to be loved by him—or at least keep peace with him. How could I trust my views when everyone else saw things so differently?

I would leave, and I'd be persuaded to return. I'd get out, get scared, and get back to the familiar. Each leaving became more frightening, every return increasingly demeaning and demanding. Intellectually, I knew what was happening was wrong, but emotionally, I was stuck. I told myself if I could change, become better, I could be the someone who helped *him* evolve. I could improve these crazy circumstances.

One night I felt resolute. I would leave and make it stick. I went to his basement apartment to deliver the news, unaware that he was on a three-day cocaine binge and seriously sleep-deprived. Me leaving him was not part of his plan. Our epic fight quickly turned crazy. He threatened me, letting me know he had a knife and could use it if I tried to leave. When he finally passed out, I escaped through a ground-level window. I was wearing a flimsy nightgown, and my purse was still in the apartment. I was so panicked that I hadn't even thought to grab my car keys.

Fortunately, a backpack in my car, full of schoolbooks, also contained a spare set of keys. I broke the window to get into my car. I didn't have my purse, but it didn't really matter. I'd given my last $200 to Joe the night before so we could keep partying. I had no money for gas or anything else. I found a few coins to make a phone call. I fled to a girlfriend's house, and she persuaded me to call my dad, to whom I'd defended Joe time and again, to whom I'd lied about where I'd been going and what I'd been doing. Even so, my girlfriend said, "You can always go home."

I told my dad I'd had a big, final fight with Joe, had no money, no place to live, and asked him to come get me. His mindset was that if I had a fight with my partner, he should send me back to my partner. In that moment, he didn't summon up kindness; he opted to be the disciplinarian he thought he should be. He made it clear no bailout was forthcoming, only one of his favorite clichés: "You made your bed, and you can lie in it."

Finally, I called a trusted counselor who knew someone across the state willing and able to help me. "If you can get to Sioux City, you can get help for your codependency and see if you have addictions." He gave me a number to call. The counselor I spoke to was supportive, promising, "Get here, and we will help you." The next call was to my brother, asking if he would give me a ride. He took me as far as he could, and I hitchhiked the rest of the way.

In Sioux City, I met with people in recovery, got involved in meetings, and lived in a halfway house for women. It was a good temporary respite, but in order to live there, I was asked to subscribe to a whole set of beliefs, including religious beliefs, with which I wasn't comfortable. It felt like going from one master to another.

On one of our house outings, we'd gone to Lake Yankton. It was beautiful and serene. Looking out at the water, I felt something shift. I sat on the shore and cried and cried, pouring my heartache into the lake. I wanted to live there. I decided I would.

It was April and the weather was getting to be fine. I had earned a little money doing odd jobs, babysitting and waiting tables. I'd gotten my admittedly crappy car back, but it worked. I set aside thoughts that it might not be safe for a young girl to camp out there alone, and used my money to buy a tent, a cooler, a few supplies, and a bunch of used spiritual and self-help books. Then I went to the lake and set up camp. Technically, it cost four dollars a day for a campsite, but a kind-hearted ranger rarely made me pay. I subsisted on a daily hamburger and fries at a little café by the campsite, and bought cold cuts, fruits, and vegetables for the cooler from the nearby market when I could afford them. While I was living in the tent, I started an internship at a treatment center so I could finish my degree. Happily, my office was in a former patient room at a hospital, so I had access to a shower and could keep a spare outfit or two there.

While my circumstances might have looked bleak to others, it was a rich time for me. At the campsite, I became part of a community, people who invited me to sit by their fires and engaged me in deep conversations. My books were reawakening me to profound truths I felt like I'd always known but had forgotten. I had plenty of time for meditating, reflecting, writing in my journal.

During the day, I was among others in recovery, doing their own personal work, striving to become good people. We talked and sang together. I was often in settings with indigenous people and with others who lived in a spiritual community called Hutterites. I felt a spiritual awakening as I studied their ways. It dawned on me that if I wanted to be something, it was up to me. I got really clear about my part in this whole dance, and I started to work through some limiting beliefs. No one needed to empower me; I could step into the power I already had. Through this experience, I began to understand that attachment causes suffering. It's not reality but rather our stories that cause suffering. Our minds are not to be trusted. I began to understand the importance of moving beyond the concrete and the mind.

My possessions were few, I was living minimally, but what more did I need? The universe was there to support me.

Stress asserted itself only when I started worrying about the future. I felt shame only when I revisited the past. When I felt anxious, it became a practice to remind myself that, in this moment, I had everything I'd ever dreamed of: a home by the most beautiful lake I'd ever seen, gorgeous sunsets, incredible friends. I'd remind myself of what was real: "I'm sheltered. I'm fed. I'm safe. I'm cared for."

I didn't need a man to feel supported and loved for who I

was. I could be my authentic self, and people affirmed that they saw me as fun, kind, and loving. When I look at pictures of myself back then, I am stunning—tanned, glowing, and happy. It was the freest I have ever felt.

As the days began to get shorter and colder, I moved back to Sioux City into an apartment, continued waiting tables, and enrolled in college to get a second degree in social work. Soon I would meet the man I would marry. We had a wonderful wedding, four incredible sons, and satisfying careers—but without the fairy-tale ending. In the many years since that young girl lived at the lake, I have had need to return to the water more than once.

Even so, my twenty-one-year-old self began a journey of evolution that, a few decades later, finds me here, staring at the water on a cool, sunny day in Mexico. I came here as a retreat from "the enemy," but I know I have brought the enemy with me. Because the enemy is the ego, the forgetting, the mind that lives on illusions and seeks quick, easy fixes.

Throughout my life, I have worked with many coaches, guides, and gurus—including that great teacher called Life Experience—and I know the imperative of seeing and accepting reality. Doing my own deeply personal work, along with helping clients over the years, has underscored the importance of being accountable for my life and my choices. I have created philosophies and strategies that help me understand and reject the dramatic stories my ego is constantly serving up. These practices are what I will turn to now.

When my practice is strong, I find happiness even in circumstances that easily could have depressed and derailed me, including the loss of both parents, followed shortly by the untimely death of my closest sibling. I've faced down infertility, obesity, divorce, single motherhood, parenting eight teenagers, and managing a large, blended family. As a female executive and business owner working in a male-dominated profession, I've achieved great success, but I've also managed to stay centered in the face of being broke, homeless, and alone.

Many people have heard versions of my reality-based philosophies in a workplace setting as a coach, trainer, or speaker. In more than two decades of working in organizational arenas, I've discovered that people have a deep hunger for my messages of unconventional wisdom, which have helped them ditch drama, accept reality, and develop self-reflective strategies that lead to improving their lives and finding satisfaction and peace. Time and time again, I get feedback that my philosophies, ideas, and tools have improved their work lives. Those who embrace my work frequently tell me that their lives outside of work have changed profoundly as well.

"When are you going to write a book that shows us how to live these principles and practices outside of work?"

I have been asked this question more times than I can count. This book is the answer. Along with strategies, practices, and tips, it is filled with stories about how I practice what I preach— and what happens when I don't. I am a living example of how, by accepting reality and making choices accordingly, anyone can stay positive and live happy no matter what their circumstances are.

At this moment, in Mexico, the sun's ascent has finally removed the morning chill, and the waves are still crashing. In the distance, I can see whales making their way south. So many visits to the water, always a return to the books, times of reflection, the relearning of lessons. Surrender. Every time, the water welcomes me home, the prodigal daughter with the messy life, reconnecting me to source and wisdom.

Yep, my life is definitely messy again, and it is getting messier even as I write this book.

My body is buzzing with the uneasiness of it, but like that twenty-one-year-old who lived by the lake, I know I have everything I need. Even as I'm pinned to the walls of the Silly Silo, I can find feelings of excitement and contentment and a sense of thrill for the future.

This book won't be about strategies to make your life less messy but instead is designed to help you walk through the messiness of life more skillfully. I want to share practices that will help you find peace even when you're in pain. It's another reason I've been called back to the water. It's time for me to share my stories.

I turn to my friend on the balcony.

"I remember that girl," I tell her. "At least today I'm looking at a way bigger lake, and I have a much better tent." We laugh.

There are so many things I wish I could go back and say to that young woman living on the edge of Lake Yankton. Instead, I'd like to say them to you. Because I want to share all the things that have taught me the most important life lesson I've discovered: You really can live happy—even when your life appears to be a mess.

PART ONE

LIVING HAPPY

TRUTH WILL SET YOU FREE

On a sacred mountain in Tecate, Mexico, I am the hiking guide for a group of successful leaders from all over the United States. It's a warm, late-spring day in 2009. Century plants are bursting into bloom like popcorn on a hot flame. The view is spectacular, the company superb, and I'm feeling like I just won the work-life lottery.

Out of the corner of my eye, I spot something ahead, slithering across the path.

SNAKE!

In an instant, with one thought, the glorious feeling I'd been experiencing blew up. The panic was instant. I began breathing heavily, it felt as though my major organs were shutting down, and the urge to pee like a pack mule was overwhelming. My mind raced. How could I survive a snakebite on a mountain? All I could come up with was a technique I remembered from a John Wayne movie—not savvy but all I had. He'd heroically whipped out a knife, cut an X over the fang marks in his hand,

and sucked out the snake venom. I reached for my pocketknife, preparing to perform self-surgery and save my own life.

Wait. No way would I be able to suck venom out of my own ankle. That's when I knew: I was going to die.

I summoned the will to take a few tentative steps forward. The huge, venomous snake was . . . well, it was a piece of rope that had fallen off someone's saddlebag. I felt relief that I would live, but I still needed to pee like a pack mule.

What was the cause of my stress? What almost ruined my beautiful moment in the mountains? What almost ended my life? A piece of rope?

Nope. It was my story about the rope. I created that story and wholeheartedly believed it. My story centered on fear: False Events Appearing Real. That part of the brain I call ego told me a tale that the rope was a snake. I believed the story, and my suffering began.

The reality of that morning was that I was healthy and hiking with a group of wonderful people in an amazing natural setting. When I saw "the snake," reality didn't change, but my story did. The story moved me from heaven to hell as my feelings of contentment and bliss disappeared. In one second, I went from thinking "This is the best job in the world" to "They can't pay me enough to do this job!" And I believed that thought without even questioning it.

When I later realized that the *story* was causing my pain, not reality, I suddenly understood something I had been witnessing my entire life. For example, when I was a child, I witnessed the pain of my parents divorcing. What ruined their marriage? Well, my mom passionately believed a story: SHE was right.

And my dad was emphatic about his story: HE was right. Each believed what their thoughts were telling them: "I AM RIGHT!" And that story trumped any desire to be happy in their marriage. How sad a story is that?

I also saw ego-based stories' role in suffering as a graduate student doing research on workplace drama. Doctors were asked to switch to a computerized patient documentation system and were given training. Simple. But instead of accepting a new reality, they created and believed stories that the change would limit their ability to care for patients. Rather than seeing an opportunity to improve patient care, the doctors told themselves change was a burden. They created a story of being victimized.

The stories we create and believe will direct our actions. In the doctors' case, instead of investing in learning and becoming fluent in new technology, they spent their time complaining and resisting. Not only did those actions have the potential to jeopardize their careers, the possibility of affecting their patients' health was also very real. The change was mandated, and it happened. Doctors began using the new system, but in the process of confronting a new reality, they created unnecessary suffering.

SELF-IMPOSED SUFFERING

That morning on the mountain in Mexico, when the story of the snake was superseded by the reality of a rope, something important clicked for me. I realized clearly that suffering is optional and mostly self-imposed.

Stress and suffering don't come from reality, they come from the stories we make up about reality. Of course, painful things happen. Pain is part of life. But the drama in stories we create in the wake of pain causes the suffering we complain about.

What might happen if you stopped believing everything you think? What if observing your thoughts was followed with a pause, stepping back with questions, and self-reflection? Employing these simple actions allows you to bypass ego and access the best part of your brain. The simple act of self-reflection is the ultimate drama diffuser and is an effective way to eliminate suffering.

My first career was counseling, talking with people one-on-one. As promotions at work led to leadership roles, I saw the ways emotional energy expended on believing the ego's stories results in drama and tremendous wastes of emotional energy. I felt so passionately about helping people see this that I invented a new career—drama researcher—because I wanted to quantify the waste and help folks reduce suffering in their lives by living drama-free.

My research put a number on the time people at work lose to drama: 2.5 hours per day. That's 150 minutes daily that's gone—poof!—lost in unproductivity. Two and a half hours of your day equals 816 precious hours a year spent in self-inflicted pain. We seek to relieve the daily pain with big doses of venting, complaining, gossiping. We invest energy in trying to figure out why that colleague is so lazy and why the boss is a control-freak jerk.

You know what's worse than the lost time? Believing you're at the mercy of circumstances. Seeing insult where none exists. Feeling miserable because you want control and can't have it. Wallowing in victimhood.

I call those perceptions, when you focus on everything that sucks, living in "low self." You feel bad. Everyone around you feels bad. It's a pretty terrible place to be, and yet we choose to go there. Every. Single. Day. That's the bad news.

The good news is that it doesn't have to be that way.

CHIPPING AWAY AT THE PIECES

After carving one of his masterpieces, the statue of David, Michelangelo supposedly was asked, "Was it hard carving such an amazing statue?"

His reply: "No, it wasn't hard at all. I simply removed anything from the marble that wasn't David."

What might life be if instead of searching for happiness or working hard to be more innovative, you realized you already were those things? What if happiness and success are your natural state once you shed the drama? All you have to do is chip away the things that aren't you.

Imagine a toggle switch, right there in the middle of your head. When it is toggled down, you see the world through the ego's lens. Circumstances are the source of your suffering. You are the victim of reality. You try to make yourself feel better by judging, venting, tattling, scorekeeping. Low self.

When you are toggled up, you can see the world differently. Compassion rises. You choose to help rather than judge. You are full of ideas and see options that allow you to have an impact in the world. Say hello to your high self. In this toggle setup, you can't be in low-self and high-self at the same time. It is impossible to be truly helpful when you're in judgment mode.

How do you flip your own toggle switch? With self-reflection—the ultimate drama defuser. You can't vent and self-reflect simultaneously. In fact, venting is the ego's way of *avoiding* self-reflection. The best way to bypass the ego—the story, the judgment, the suffering—is self-reflection.

Over time, I discovered three simple questions that have been crucial to initiate self-reflection and set myself free from suffering.

Question 1: What Do I Know for Sure?

This question almost instantly helps release the ego's clench on my worldview. Without changing anything, it changes everything. Suddenly a micromanaging boss becomes a manager who prefers more detail than I like to give. An idea from someone else is something to think about, not something that ruins everything I have worked for. The militant DMV employee trying to ruin my dang life becomes someone who informs me the office is closing for the day and lets me know when I can return to renew my license.

The ex-husband trying to wrest my children away from me becomes a dad asking for an extra day with his kids.

In all these cases, reality wasn't causing pain. The stories about my circumstances that I'd chosen to believe created suffering—like that day on the mountain where I almost lost my life to a piece of poisonous rope.

Focusing on what you know for sure, rather than what your low-self tells you, means reflecting on what's happening and seeing reality for what it is. Rarely is reality as bad as it seems.

I remember asking a nurse working on a full unit at a hospital how things were going one day. He said, "Oh, things are crazy. They're just totally, totally crazy."

I said, "Really, is that true? Are things really crazy? I know they're busy, but are things really wildly unmanageable? Where did the crazy part come from?"

He thought for a second and said, "Oh, dang, I added that . . . You know, you're right. It really is just busy. I added the crazy part."

I asked him if adding the crazy to his story was helpful. He laughed and said, "No. Not at all."

When I answer Question 1, the toggle is easier to switch up. I can stop judging and begin to see reality more clearly. I gain more peace and energy. I find the room for compassion to grow. When that happens, my natural inclination is to help, which blooms into . . .

Question 2: What Can I Do to Help?

I can reflect on what I could do to enhance my boss's trust in me, to make it easier for my former husband to see the kids, to actually be nice to the helpful DMV employee and return to renew my license during regular hours.

Asking "How can I help?" moves me beyond my ego and often leads friends, coworkers, and family members to spontaneously do the same. For example, I have a wonderful sister who never had children of her own, which left her a lot of time to worry about our siblings, my kids, and the kids of our siblings.

One day she called to talk about our brother. "Cy, did you hear about Michael?"

The way she asked signaled we might be headed for a trip to low-self town.

I said, "Michael? I love that guy! What's up?"

She let loose: "He's buying a house he can't afford, which means he's going to be destitute in retirement because his wife, you know, has caviar tastes on a Meow Mix budget . . ." On and on.

When she finally took a breath, I jumped in.

"Wow, I love Michael. I would hate for him not to have what he needs in retirement. What can I do to help? What should *we be doing* to help?" Then I started brainstorming. "I know, I have extra money, maybe I'll just send him some. If he's destitute in retirement? He can come live with me."

My questions shifted the energy. My sister backed up: "I'm not getting involved with that hot mess." I immediately replied, "Okay, sounds good, so what would you like to do for the holidays?"

When my sister saw that the conversation based on her judgment of my brother's choices wouldn't be productive, we moved on without me having to ask that we move on. A simple "How can I help?" toggled the switch.

Using these two questions, I lived a few years in what seemed like bliss. I felt so enlightened! Sure, I would get tripped up when my ego argued, "Yeah, but I shouldn't have to help in this situation." But usually the price to be helpful was small, so I did it anyway.

One night in Chicago, however, I was in a situation where the two questions didn't lead me to where I needed to go. From a place deep inside, a final self-reflective question emerged.

Question 3: What Would Great Look Like?

Let's face it—sometimes reality *is* painful. You lose a job. Someone says something that feels unkind and so you give it that label. Someone disappoints you. The job you wanted goes to someone else. Your child gets sick. Your loved one dies. Reality can hurt. Our low selves want to wallow there, to stay stuck in victimhood and also to complain about it because, you know, it just isn't right!

That's the state I was in one evening in Chicago.

The man I had loved dearly for twenty-three years had made choices that ended our marriage. Five years earlier, he had broken his neck and nearly drowned after diving into a pool and hitting his head. In the darkness, I dove in and saved him. I stood by him through a long rehabilitation, determined to build a new life for us. And he recovered.

And then he left us. Me and our four young sons. I was devastated, scared, and, at times, desperate.

The separation was brutal. Though he had recovered, his head injury fueled fury and blame for me. As I would learn during our divorce proceedings, he was focused on the division of assets with a goal of ensuring that I wouldn't get more than what he had determined was my fair share.

Even so, my life wasn't completely horrible—it was a mixed bag, as life usually is. Good things also were happening. I was launching a new career; it was going better than expected. And I had been invited to give the biggest keynote address of my life to a large, important audience. A golden opportunity.

That was the situation when I arrived at a swanky hotel in Chicago. I was giddy with anticipation and excitement. My plan was to check in, get a great night's sleep, look like a million bucks the next day, and wow folks from the stage.

I pulled up in my rental car and reveled in the greeting from porters who came to take my bags. I walked to the registration desk for check in.

My credit card was declined. What? No worries! Here's another! Declined. And still another: declined.

My husband, it appeared, had maxed out our joint credit cards to secure assets. I had no money, which meant no place to stay for the night. I was panicked and furious. My big day tomorrow! He was taking it from me! This wasn't just my story, it felt like my reality! I was supporting all of us, raising the boys, juggling home and career, running around like a madwoman to make it all work. This was really happening, and it wasn't fair. I fully believed those thoughts and almost gave up.

With my ego working overtime, I turned to the first two questions. What did I know for sure? My story was that my husband was trying to destroy me and drive me to financial ruin! In that moment, it felt like I knew this for sure. How could I help? In that moment, I couldn't see how he possibly could deserve help! He had taken actions that threatened to ruin my beautiful opportunity! No matter how hard I tried, I was unable to see past what was happening and find the clarity and peace these two questions usually provided. They were failing me.

And then from nowhere and from everywhere, a new question arose in my spirit.

The ultimate question: *If I were going to be great right now, what would that look like?*

Great would be succeeding in spite of these unfair circumstances—joyfully. Doing it for me, for my kids, and yes, even for him.

With that question I moved from judging, sailed right past

helping, and tapped into creativity and innovation. Nowhere to sleep? Do I know that for sure? I had a rental car and the seats folded down. Not ideal, but doable. I found a place to park and set an alarm. Look like a million bucks? Well, the hotel had a fancy spa. All I had to do was wait for a guest to enter with her key and piggyback on her entrance. That's what I did.

The keynote went great, my first book launched successfully, and my business continued to grow. Not because I muscled through, but because I peacefully rose above.

I moved beyond the conflict with my husband to a place where I could engage the world on my terms and make the impact I knew I was born to make. My high-self asked good questions: "What if I were able to succeed in spite of these circumstances? What if I were able to be *great* right now—in spite of everything? What would that look like?"

That brief personal inquiry turned the attention from myself to my vision of a better world, living my purpose, making the impact I felt called to make. Great in that situation meant being the best working mom I could be for my kids and giving them a fabulous next chapter. Great meant taking the stage, fully present to those I was there to serve, and getting my research into the workplace and the world place.

Thanks to these three questions, my ego's story lost its power. I chose to focus on what I knew for sure, help myself, and be great. Because I chose to be great in the face of daunting, painful circumstances, I have made a career based on helping others disconnect from their drama as well. Self-reflection is not about positive thinking. It's about putting your mind to work for you, not against you.

These questions have been gifts from my highest self in times of need. I want them to be my gift to you.

THREE QUESTIONS TO FIND CLARITY

1. **What do I know for sure?** This reveals your story and loosens the ego's grip. It almost always reveals a less harsh reality.

2. **How can I help?** This gets you out of victim mode and into the role of co-creator or compassionate contributor.

3. **What would great look like in this situation?** This is liberation. It shows your external circumstances don't have to drive your decisions and actions. You can live your values out loud and with integrity and live your purpose with intention instead of reaction.

BEGINNER'S GRATITUDE

Near the end of my first year in college, I was invited to my boyfriend's family Thanksgiving celebration. I was excited about being with him and his family for this holiday, one of my favorites.

I also was studying diligently for the final exam of my first psychology class, and my mind was swirling with newfound knowledge about the human tendency to see the world as a dark, scary place. I had learned that our brains evolved to ensure human survival by constantly scanning the environment for risk and danger. Basically, we are hardwired to perceive constant threat even though in the modern age, many of those existential threats no longer exist.

This revelation got me thinking about what I would eventually come to call the "religion of suffering" that we all are co-opted into at a young age. We are trained to "pre-suffer" because we anticipate terrible things that might happen in the future, and we dread them in the present. And in the wake of life's inevitable pain, we often cling to it and keep suffering alive. This happens, at least in part, because of our natural human condition—a brain function called ego.

These thoughts swirled in the background of my college-student head as I gathered with my boyfriend's family and friends around the Thanksgiving dinner table. There, I witnessed a ritual that altered the direction of the swirl and helped change the way I see the world. Before we began eating, his parents announced they had composed a list of things for which they were thankful. They held up a piece of paper. We looked expectantly. The paper was blank. Nothing to see.

I was confused.

His folks then carefully held the paper just above the candles burning on the dinner table. Magically, the flame revealed words. Heat illuminated their list of blessings. My boyfriend's parents' invisible ink trick sparked beautiful reflections around the table. The discussion centered on how the gifts and graces we experience daily feel so common that they become invisible. Sometimes it takes extra effort, even a little "heat," to see them.

At the end of the dinner, they put the paper on the refrigerator, where it would be on display until the next holiday gathering. I was moved.

SHARPENING MY GRATITUDE VISION

This list of "invisible" blessings made me think about the possibilities of training my brain to see what might not be immediately visible. While I had learned the brain attended to survival by focusing on the negative, maybe it could be rewired to override that natural tendency by consciously seeking out the positive. Maybe deliberate gratitude was a way to create a different perspective, even when I was feeling under fire or experiencing tough times. With a bit more focus, I could surely always find some little thing for which to be thankful.

Creating a gratitude practice seemed like a practical way to do the trick. Ever the overachiever, I decided to gratitude big. I bought the Oprah-recommended gratitude journal, purchased fancy pens and dressed up the pages with elaborate doodles, sketches, artwork, and cool photos clipped from magazines. This new practice worked like a charm. I became more positive, and I could more readily see—put a name to—all the good things happening in my life. With dedication to this practice, my worldview shifted.

As I contemplated and practiced gratitude over time, my views slowly evolved. First, I had begun seeing and naming my blessings. But after a while, just naming what I was grateful for seemed a little muted and pale. One of my yoga teachers, Paul Gould, often says, "Where you put your attention determines the quality of your life." In one yoga class I attended, he talked about the ways that counting your blessings can create attachment and craving. It's easy to acknowledge what we have and then begin immediately scanning the horizon for what's next. I thought about how focusing on an accumulation of blessings, rather than sitting with and enjoying the awe of them, was a form of devaluing the gifts I had been given.

Because I wasn't reflecting deeply on what I had with thorough appreciation and enjoyment, my practice felt transactional. Perhaps I was just keeping score, accumulating gratitude points. With mindful attention to what I had in the moment, my awareness and appreciation of its worth increased. Mindfully appreciating the blessing actually quelled my craving for more. Savoring what I had increased its value and sparked the recognition that I had plenty. I became conscious of the fact that I was fully nurtured. What I had was enough. More than enough.

When I took the time to be truly present with my gratitude, the volume amplified. I really, really smelled those roses! And smelling the roses became so satisfying that, in the moment, smelling roses was all I needed to be content. Maybe that's an exaggeration. Food and shelter and a nice glass of wine were pretty great, too. But my new focus on mindful gratitude felt like a decluttering, like walking in a Zen garden and soaking in the simplicity, or being in retreat, where you are given only what you really need. I felt satisfied and fulfilled.

In time, this mindful gratitude moved me naturally to a place of humility. The refocused practice forced me to acknowledge that so much of what I had received wasn't even earned. My brilliance or efforts didn't create the reward. I was blessed beyond what I deserved. Blessings were offered to me, easily plucked like ripe, nourishing fruit from a tree. Literally, gifts bestowed by a benevolent universe.

This humility crystallized as I prepared for an interview with a woman who hosted a streaming radio show (the precursor to today's podcasts). I was a relatively young, new entrepreneur about to launch my first book. I knew good PR was one way to boost book sales and grow my business. We had sent publicity pitches to various media outlets, and this one landed. A radio host asked to interview me, which looked like a great opportunity to get ex-

posure for the book and the work I did. The idea was to talk
about my fabulously successful career and tell the world all my
tips and secrets for accomplishing a successful life. She sent a list
of questions in advance of the interview so I could prepare.

The first question was something like, "What do you love
about being an entrepreneur and founder? What are the positive benefits?" Easy. I grabbed my gratitude lists and looked for
anything that had to do with being an entrepreneur.

But the next questions felt more challenging. How did I create my own opportunities? How did I conquer my field? What
did I do to win? How did I outsmart people? How did I know
when to zig, when to zag? How did I do it? What was my secret
for success?

Digging for answers, I thought about how much I loved the
work I did, in my chosen field. I could craft my own day, and I
worked with great people. But how did I do it? Answers eluded
me because I was realizing that I hadn't done it. Yes, I showed
up. I prepared, and I worked hard. But in good faith, I could
not claim a "secret," nor could I really take credit for the life I
had. Claiming "the win" meant making something up or revising
history.

I really wanted the exposure this radio show might bring me.
But looking for authentic answers to many of her questions was
creating an existential crisis. It struck me that most of what I
had was a result of accepting opportunities offered. I was invited, and I eagerly accepted the invitations. My amazing team
carried out much of the work of the business. I had help in writing my book. And I wrote a book because an agent who'd seen
my blog thought I had a book in me. My beautiful, comfortable

house had been built by others, and the money I used to pay the mortgage came from what other people paid me.

The cognitive dissonance these interview questions created for me was a little haunting. I wanted to grow my audience and my client list. My ego was screaming, "Are you crazy?! Your life is good, and damn right you made it happen. Take the credit!" But in the purest place of my heart, I knew that just wasn't the case. I could not rewrite history. How could I not recognize that other people and not-so-random circumstances had heavily contributed to paving my successful path? I couldn't travel back in time and add intentionality. The world wanted me to take credit for where I was, but my insight said I needed to take *less* credit. People had given me keys to open doors—or sometimes left the door propped wide open. I had to acknowledge that the true source of what I had wasn't mine to claim.

I'm not saying I sat around eating peeled grapes while someone delivered my great life on a shining silver platter. I am ambitious and conscientious and a hard worker. But in reviewing my gratitude lists, I also had to acknowledge that many other people with intelligence, talent, and a work ethic didn't have equal access to the same opportunities and advantages that I had. Many people didn't have the same privilege. As my dad frequently used to say, "There but for the grace of God go I."

These reflections broke my heart open. I had to wonder if my gratitude list was little more than hash marks of "good life" points. As I wrestled with the implications of the true source of my blessings, my gratitude practice was evolving: First see positive in my life. Second, acknowledge the true source of the positive blessings—my grace and my privilege.

And then I was faced with another dilemma: If I recognized that I have abundance because of privilege, should I find ways to live with less privilege? Was I supposed to feel guilty about what I had? Find a way to live smaller? Donate everything I had to the poor? This was no small struggle. I really like small luxuries and incredible experiences. Living the good life brings me great pleasure. I had bought a Louis Vuitton bag after my first book contract; should I not have done so? (I love that bag, continue to use it today, and it still brings me joy!)

Or maybe the call to action was something different. My question became, "If everyone else can't write a list like mine, why not? And how can I find a way to do for others what has been done for me?"

Maybe what was called for was maintaining gratitude, courting humility, and marrying those two things to focused generosity. Maybe I could hang on to, and savor, the things and experiences for which I was grateful and also allow them to define greater purpose. I had been given so much, and this insight fueled a motivation to do what I could to help others compile gratitude lists that were as varied and abundant as mine is.

Over the years I've looked for ways to do that. Sometimes the ways to give back find me. Several years ago, for instance, I was asked to serve on a board. Normally my instinctive response to being asked to be on a board is a loud, internal groan: "No . . . NO! I don't want to." Don't get me wrong. I know board members do good and important work, but it's not my preferred form of service. But when I heard about the mission of this nonprofit organization, my six-year-old self demanded that I say yes.

From the time I learned to read, I have loved books more than just about anything else. I devoured all the books I could get my hands on, including the tattered, worn books at home that had been through five siblings. When I was six, I got a library card, a golden, lifetime pass to the magic kingdom of adventure, fantasy, and knowledge. Here was access to a treasure trove of clean, fresh books, providing fodder and fire for my active mind.

Imagine the disappointment that six-year-old girl felt when she discovered the library rules limited her to two books in one week.

Only two? The librarians might as well have told me I could only eat two meals a week.

One day, the librarians pulled me aside for a chat. I remember them as being very nice, and also intimidating! They had authority. They held the keys of power. "We've noticed how much you really love books," they told me. "And we've also noticed that you take really good care of them." Because I was such a voracious reader and a conscientious caretaker of books, they had agreed to bend the rules for me. I would be allowed to check out five books a week. Five! The clouds parted, and the sun revealed the literary pot at the end of a book-lined rainbow.

Those librarians saw a need in a little girl and had the generosity to find a way to fulfill it. Because they were willing to make an exception, I was allowed to slake my perpetual thirst for reading. My reading passion has given me true wealth, the goose that consistently delivers fresh golden eggs. It's impossible to overstate the ways that reading books has contributed to the person I am.

That small-town, reading-obsessed girl grew up to become a *New York Times* best-selling author. When my first book was launched, I did a book signing event at my hometown library.

One of those librarians, now retired, showed up. She made a point to remind me about the six-year-old girl, whom she remembered well. She recounted how my love of books, and the reverent way I treated them, inspired her and her colleagues to make a dream come true. "And look at you now in this very same library," she said, "signing books that you authored."

It was soon after that my author friend asked me to take her place on that board. She told me, "I think you'll like this organization. It's called Delivering Infinite Book Shelves." Its mission is to support teachers and encourage children's love of reading through abundance. Because of the work DIBS does, students are able to choose and take home a fresh book each and every school night—five books a week.

I had the opportunity to open a door that had been opened for me, and I wasn't about to say "no" to helping kids alter their worlds in the way mine had been. To do otherwise would feel irresponsible.

For me, gratitude and giving back is much like breathing— receive the inhale and you are nourished; in the exhale, release back what you have taken in and nourish others. It's a path from gratitude to aligned action. It's a way to find humility in your own abundance and privilege and to find compassion and generosity for others. It provides motivation to ensure others have cause for gratitude as well.

Gratitude fused with generosity expands the blessing. A practice of gratitude that fuels generosity can change other people's lives in an impactful way. Breathe in gratitude, breathe out generosity. Repeat.

A vital, virtuous cycle.

LIVING GRATITUDE OUT LOUD

Here is a practice to take you from gratitude to sustainable generosity, from attitude to action:

- If you don't keep a gratitude list, start one.

- Review your list. Be present with what you've captured. See it.

- Name it. Appreciate its value. Savor it.

- Understand its true source. Where did the thing for which you are grateful really come from? Is there a gap between what you earned and what was given?

- If it was a blessing bestowed, think about others who might not be able to put something similar on their gratitude lists. Let your heart be broken open by the random or structured way our current world blesses some but not others.

- Recognize your privilege. Let it humble you.

- Find and nurture compassion.

- Let your gratitude list inspire action to "fill the gap" between what you have and what others lack access to or don't have.

- Ask yourself, "How can I help ensure that everyone has gratitude lists as rich and satisfying as mine?"

GRATITUDE 2.0: MAY "THANK YOU" BE MY ONLY PRAYER

My life has had times of great prosperity, and I also have lost almost everything—more than once. When my first marriage ended, I took on more than a million dollars in debt, offset by no collateral, in exchange for ensuring custody of my children so I could raise them in a safe, stable place. Among the things that got me through that incredibly messy time was my initial gratitude practice, writing those daily lists of things that made me feel good or gave me hope. This helped me to keep the faith, to keep going. I wrote down acts of kindness, small and large. I noted grace and generosity I experienced that, at times, stopped me in my tracks. I wrote about things that appeared without even asking: a check received the moment before desperation set in, a referral that boosted business, a sweet evening cuddling in the arms of a new love.

As I focused on the positive, my life felt happier. My attention and awe unveiled miracles happening to me daily. While my happiness wasn't dependent on the happenings of the day, I did feel happier when I reviewed the many things for which I could be grateful. Refining my worldview and turning up the volume of my appreciation inspired me to share my abundance in impactful and gratifying ways. In a very real sense, it restored my faith in the universe.

But as I overcame obstacles and experienced success again, my practice veered into something else. When I'm on the achievement path, sometimes old thinking asserts itself. I became superstitious. I began "performing" for the universe. What if I weren't really worthy of this abundance? Fear begin to whisper that if I weren't appreciative enough, like *super* appreciative, blessings might be withheld.

It took me a while to notice, but I got stuck.

THERE IS SUPERSTITION

Seeing the positive things in my life was an improvement, but even so, my view had become limited. It started to feel like all the low-hanging fruit from the gratitude tree had been harvested. Soon I was viewing my life through a lens of what could make the list, hash marks made for the sake of the tally. I was really good at counting blessings, but I started to feel disturbed at the judgment involved in creating my lists. By naming something in order to add it to the tally, it somehow made the experience a little pale, less interesting, and placed it outside of mystery and possibility.

It became transactional: count blessings, consider privilege, give accordingly. The lists weren't inspiring the satisfaction and joy I once had felt. Instead, they became a way to ward off evil or loss. If I didn't capture something good on my list, the universe might consider me ungrateful and snatch it away—again. It was a little like negotiating, or even blackmail—pay the price or lose something precious. My once-effortless practice had become a mental gratitude treadmill, which I faithfully climbed on every day accompanied by a slight fear that I might fall off.

The ego—watch out for this—is clever, sophisticated, and persistent. It saw an opening and co-opted my gratitude practice. I began to suspect the habit that had led me to transcend a negative view of life was morphing into my prison guard, led by my ego. I needed more transcendence. But what could I transcend to?

THE PROBLEM OF DUALITY

For years, I had done a nightly list, even if I had to scribble it late at night on a bar napkin. I felt uncomfortable going to bed unless I ticked that box because I might wake up the next morning and find it gone. I was afraid to piss off the universe. My negotiations with the universe were about "earning" what I was given. I thought about the ways my practice had gone stale and noticed the infusion of anxiety.

I had heard from many teachers who taught about the universal principles of ending suffering that peace and happiness come to those who can move from counting blessings to counting *everything* as a blessing. Deeper reflection helped me realized that my list was all about the "good."

My practice had started in peace, a way to see the positive in my life, but it had mutated into a daily negotiation between my ego and the universe, my ego and God. I had incarcerated myself in a prison of duality.

By rating an event or an object as a blessing, I was subtly rejecting significant parts of my day or my life. When circumstances unfolded as I preferred, that was eagerly accepted. But tagging along with my warm welcome of the preferred was a low-grade anxiety that it might not stay or come again—my version of attachment. My notes to the universe said, "Here are the blessings I am attached to."

Looking with new eyes, I realized my lists reeked of judgment. My ego was creating stories about what was "good" in my life, which were a statement of my life preferences. It was like an offering to the cosmos to keep blessings coming. I would be faithful in my gratitude practice, and the universe would give me a lot to be grateful for—deal?

But my judgments and labels obscured something important. Every welcomed development of the day contained a foretelling of inevitable loss. Labeling "good" and "bad" ensnared me in duality, an unnecessary tension created by thinking everything falls into one category or another. My ego carved out the whole complex experience of life into buckets of "positive" components and "negative" parts.

Duality thinking, with its premature, short-sighted judgment, imprisons us on a roller coaster of intense feelings and reactivity. It disrupts authentic gratitude. My gratitude lists were out of alignment with my faith in the vastness and possibilities of the universe.

Fostering wholehearted gratitude would require me to reconfigure my vision to break the duality habit and see the whole. I wanted to stop fragmenting and labeling the circumstances in my life. What would happen if I stopped "cherry-picking" gratitude?

I thought about an old Buddhist morality tale—many versions exist—but the one I remember centers on a poor farmer. He meets his circumstances with equanimity while his neighbors ride the roller coaster of duality.

The farmer, with gratitude for his old horse's hard work and service, sets it free in the mountains to live life in peace. Neighbors, seeing the man pulling his own plow, immediately judge his circumstance: "What a shame you have no horse. How unfortunate!" The farmer replies, "Good? Bad? Who knows?"

The horse, rejuvenated from feeding on wild, green grasses in the meadows, returns to the farmer accompanied by a dozen feral, healthy horses. The villagers congratulate him on his unexpected good fortune: "How happy you must be!" But the farmer replies, "Good? Bad? Who knows?"

The farmer's only son, who attempts to train one of the wild horses, is seriously injured. The villagers, seeing only duality, bemoan the farmer's plight. "What tragedy! Now your son can't help on the farm." The farmer replies with his mantra of neutrality: "Good? Bad? Who knows?"

War breaks out, and the emperor demands that young, healthy men must fight. The farmer's injured son avoids the war. "How lucky you are!" cry the villagers as their sons leave to fight.

Clearly, the tale could go on and on. Good? Bad? Who knows? The neighbors were on an emotional roller coaster, expressing judgments based on duality. The farmer didn't waste his energy. He claimed the neutrality of the universe's actions. By refusing to label things good or bad, the farmer remained open, curious, confident—free from the duality trap. He embraced the whole of life.

I realized duality thinking had me stuck on a level of suffering and exhaustion with a lot of free-flowing anxiety on the side. A gratitude list with a narrow vision of "good" can only be thin and obscured. Experiences deemed "bad" ignore unforeseen benefits and inherent growth in store from a kind universe. Transcending duality isn't just an exercise in thinking positively or ignoring a large part of the total experience. And it isn't just about looking for the silver lining—you have to look at, accept, and appreciate the entire cloudscape.

KEEPING FAITH

The fears and anxiety that began to take root in my early gratitude practice were a crisis of faith. If I believe a kind universe truly has my back—and I do—then performing and negotiating were expressions of lost faith.

I could have conserved so much energy and avoided a lot of suffering and heartbreak over my life if I'd had the wisdom of the farmer. In moments of pain and disappointment, I failed to appreciate that the blessing might come from what happens next. If gratitude came at all, it came later, with 20/20 hindsight. My first, limited view of what I call the Great Australian Adventure is a case in point.

As a budding organizational consultant with a young family, I was offered something I saw as "good"—an opportunity to work and live in Australia for a year or more. The training I'd done for a large, international business had generated great enthusiasm. Senior managers wanted to roll it out companywide. I was pregnant with my third son, so long back-and-forth flights weren't feasible. My limited thinking was "Well, I can't work with them until my kids are older. Oh, well."

But company leaders were eager to make it work and came up with an innovative solution: Skip the flying back and forth and start work right after my son was born. They suggested I move to Australia for several months and work full-time. The company would pay for my relocation, and I'd get a terrific salary for the year. Fantastic! This was my proof that by dreaming big, I could manifest something great.

It didn't take much to persuade my husband, who also loved to travel. We loved the idea of our young children living in a new environment overseas. With great anticipation and excitement, we said "YES!" I heartily approved of the way things were going.

We were dreaming and scheming big, and our families, children, colleagues, and friends were supportive. I began shutting down my consulting practice. Not a big risk—I'd be making plenty of money. Two lucrative contracts and my intellectual property went to my colleagues. We would rent our house to friends. My husband requested a transfer with his company to a different role in Australia. We began downsizing our lives. Good? You bet!

Then, seemingly out of the blue, a senior manager in Australia called with devastating news. A corporation had purchased the company, and all training was on hold. Maybe permanently. Just like that, my big, beautiful dream vanished. In my view, this was nothing but bad. The disappointment and humiliation felt visceral. In addition to emotional devastation, the company's decision had huge ramifications for me, personally, professionally, and financially.

As a new consultant, I hadn't protected myself with a cancellation clause in the contract we'd negotiated. My once-thriving business was now nonexistent. I'd given away lucrative contracts, and no one offered to give them back. I felt resentful. The friends who were counting on renting our home had to scramble to find a place to live. My husband told me he felt betrayed and that he wouldn't easily trust me again. He had invested in my dream, and it hadn't worked out. It was a tough time in our marriage.

The mess was pervasive, and I had friends and family who were all too happy to collude with me in seeing the situation as bad. I invested large amounts of emotional energy thinking of ways to nail this horrible company to the wall for taking a big dump on my beautiful dream.

A couple of months later, I got a call from my mom, who then was in her sixties. More bad news: a lump in her breast, requisite tests, a cancer diagnosis. The doctors recommended a mastectomy. Mom assured me there was no need to come home. My sister, Lorann, would be her caregiver. "You don't need to be here for the surgery," they both insisted. "Nothing you can do."

But I went anyway. And while I was there, my sister was not herself. She was angry, dismissive, snapped at the slightest provocation. She finally blurted out that she also had a lump in her breast. She was terrified. As Mom recovered from her surgery, my sister, Mom's caregiver, was diagnosed with two types of breast cancer. She needed a double mastectomy.

In the space of a few weeks, our family was hit with two

bomb diagnoses of deadly cancer. It felt like another pile on. My life was already in a turmoil of financial and career uncertainty, I had two toddlers and a newborn, and now the cosmos was dumping another layer of mess on me. Even so, in the moment, I had a clear thought that maybe I should put my personal problems aside and be present for my loved ones.

While two family members battling cancer felt plenty bad, I also felt plenty grateful to be there for them during this family crisis. While losing that contract didn't stop feeling like a devastation, the loss gave me time and proximity to spend a lot of time with my mom. I was able to be there for her and my sister in a way I couldn't have been if I'd been living in Australia.

I had been throwing all these fits, allowing disappointment, sadness, and anger to color my life. As I had heard my mom say countless times in her life: "If it doesn't turn out okay in the end, it's not the end." And it did turn out okay—I got the gift, a blessing, of being there for my family.

In retrospect, I see how I had allowed myself to get stuck in duality because of the "developments of the day." I abandoned my faith that the universe is kind. I've had to relearn this lesson many times: I don't always know what's best.

I still had to process a whirlwind of feelings, but now I realize my ego's attachment to moving to Australia was the source of my suffering.

Without trust in the universe, a gratitude list can't be much more than an exercise in positive thinking, and it won't foster peaceful living. Without transcending duality and expanding my vision, gratitude will always be fleeting.

Like the farmer's neighbors, my stories would keep me on an

emotional roller coaster of "good" and "bad." I had to learn not only to love what I received but also to love the coming and the going of everything—what my teachers called impermanence.

When I am able to detach labels from events, my heart welcomes it all. And in those times that I can't yet be grateful for it all, I can commit to being grateful while it is happening. No need to worry about how it will all play out.

Transcending duality keeps me out of victimhood and makes me a better partner with the universe, with God. While it can be hard to welcome something that feels hurtful or disappointing, in that moment, the question I want to ask is "Will I let this traumatize me or evolve me?"

HONORING IMPERMANENCE

When gratitude is based on *current* value or appearance, happiness will always be dependent on external circumstances. Because whatever you have, whatever you assign value to, is guaranteed to change. What is born will surely die. The seeds of love always contain heartbreak. It doesn't make sense to put contentment in the hands of others or in forces that can't be controlled. Sustainable happiness isn't tied to the messiness or the brilliance of a perceived experience. Wholehearted gratitude means understanding and accepting impermanence, knowing that whatever you receive, you also will eventually have to let go.

My dearest friend, Cathy, was diagnosed with Stage 4 breast cancer, which meant cancer cells had spread throughout her body. After the diagnosis, she called, I came, we cried.

We met working as young leaders at a Behavioral Health

Center, and something about her made me know right away she was "my person." For more than thirty years, she had been steadfast and loving. Always loving. She had been my moral support, my partner in every corner of my life, in times of celebration and in the messiest times. I couldn't imagine my world without her.

We felt no gratitude for a cancer diagnosis, not one bit. And for a considerable time, we sat with the pain of it. We soaked in the rage, the injustice, the devastation, the grief.

Our first reactions centered on strategies to fight this deadly disease. She'd strap on war gear! If she had to go out, she'd be kicking and screaming. She'd show this disease she was no pushover. That's how people talk about cancer, right? You fight the good fight, vanquish the foe!

But the more we talked about it, the less sense it made to us. How does war ever end well? And did Cathy really want to spend whatever time she had left at war with her own body? The idea of losing her life, and me losing my dearest friend, was unbearably painful. We didn't resist that pain, but neither did we see the point of giving it a permanent home in the years to come. She wasn't dying from cancer; she was living with cancer. The bittersweet reality of being alive means it's inevitable that we will lose loved ones to illness and accidents. Death is as natural as life. We are all dying and living at the same time.

As we talked, we realized a war with cancer didn't align with who she is or how she has lived. It wasn't the frame she wanted to put around her experience. Cathy's cancer was reality. She wouldn't give up, but neither would she declare war. She would choose to have a different relationship with it.

Cathy liked the idea of a dance. She would dance with cancer and see what it had to teach her. She would be curious, ask lots of questions, and consider her options in the context of the dance. She also would look for ways to help others. While she wasn't ready to give up on her life, she was committed to giving up her resistance to what would unfold. When it was time for palliative care, she wanted to be ready, at peace, and conscious about her transition.

As we have always done in our friendship, we helped each other to avoid suffering beyond the pain of diagnosis by discussing the pointlessness of clinging to the hurt. We chose to live this chapter of our lives together full on.

Our time together while she danced with cancer was the most sacred of our thirty-year friendship. Most days we couldn't be honestly grateful for her condition, yet we were able to experience moments of deep gratitude in the midst of dancing with her cancer. We knew forever had never been promised. Instead, we focused on gratitude for our deep, long friendship and for the time we had together as she danced. That helped us to remember that not everything we lose is a loss.

ENJOY OR EVOLVE

I have come to a very different practice of gratitude. I work to reflect on and contemplate each day and to count everything as a blessing. Reality appears in three ways—and all of them are in my favor:

Experiences that are easy to love—the now, the life-affirming.

Experiences that I don't yet love because I don't know how they will turn out.

Experiences that help me evolve, that foster resiliency and get me ready for what's next.

This gratitude emanates from being fully present in the moment. It's appreciating the fullness of the experience—what I can see in real time paired with the recognition that I might not yet recognize the opportunity it holds. No matter what happens, I can be grateful for all the experiences because they affirm my faith in the universe, help me build trust, and create personal resilience.

My key to happiness now is to rejoice in all of the day, with a conscious response of gratitude that greets mystery. My gratitude is no longer a reaction to what has happened but a chosen response to what is happening. My chosen response is infused with an intention of curiosity and appreciation, which I turn to even in the midst of the most challenging times. This secures sustainable happiness, even in the messiness, with a respectful nod to the inevitability of what happens next.

CREATING A COMPLETE GRATITUDE PRACTICE

Over many years, I have developed tricks to create a more complete practice that helps me be grateful for everything. I think they are worth sharing with you. If you can develop the habit of suspending judgment, letting go of attachment, and ignoring your ego's stories about what it all means, your vision of gratitude will expand. You can experience consistent contentment.

Establish Neutrality. Events are neither good nor bad. Suffering comes from clinging to pain, creating stories, continually adding color to your commentary. If you are not grateful for what is, you're not seeing it clearly. What you thought happened in the past never did. What you think might happen next is about fear, not an accurate prediction. Edit your story down to what is real, and resistance will fade. Neutralize stories about things that wouldn't land on your traditional gratitude list with the notion that "everything is welcome here." Resist the naming that includes a statement about your ego's preference. Stay curious about what's next.

Acknowledge Impermanence. It's natural to want to hang on to what we love, but it's also a big source of suffering. We stay in relationships too long. We keep running until our poor knees become injured or disabled. We mourn because the vacation is ending. We can't bear the thought of losing our best friend to cancer. But everything changes. Something begins, and it will always end. Consider life the way you do the weather. It changes constantly, and we have no control. Sunny days and storms always pass. If I'm stuck, sometimes I realize I just need to grieve for a while, then let go. Sit with what you don't prefer, even with events that feel hard or painful. Be fully present in the moment and then let go. If you resist impermanence, suffering persists. Be as good a hostess to the experience as you would be to an unexpected but mandatory guest.

If Not Grateful For, then Grateful While. For me, the COVID-19 pandemic became an interesting take on many things being true at the same time. My intellectual response to losing millions of dollars' worth of business when bookings were suspended or canceled was "This sucks." I also was stranded in Mexico because of the pandemic, far away from my family and business, a new empty nester, at a time when I was trying to negotiate a painful divorce. But I noticed another response that also felt authentic, something that wasn't coming from my brain but felt like my true being—bliss. I had nowhere to be for months, no business to tend to, no husband, and no big responsibilities. In the midst of a global crisis, I had feelings of expectancy and excitement. It was like my insides didn't match my experience. Was I losing it? I had a conversation with a friend that helped me put things in perspective. As we caught up on our lives, she casually mentioned something she'd been mulling over: "You know," she said, "you can go through the next few months as a prisoner or as a monk." While life felt extremely messy from my house in Mexico, I also felt a kind of liberation. I had been forced to take a giant time out. If someone had told me, "Take three months off to retreat, rest, indulge in self-care, examine your schedule, see what your busy-ness is keeping you from knowing, lie around, grieve, write, and just be," I would have resisted. "I can't do that! I have family to care for and a business to run." Instead, I chose to be the monk. I didn't set goals to become something else. I chose to rest and let it be. I listened to my body. I read. I got solid in my meditation practice and used my beach walks to reflect on my life. I emerged much clearer, healthier—and fifty pounds lighter. Was I grateful for a global pandemic? No. But I was grateful for what I received because of it. I was grateful while I lived through it.

Foster a Welcoming Heart. What you can't easily be grateful for has a lot to say about where you need to let go. When something feels hard or challenging, can you, in the moment, see opportunities for growth and evolution? Is it time to release a limiting belief; trust the universe; get more skilled, willing, or ready for something new? When you can say "Yes, I am willing to see the value in all of it, even if it's not in my favor or brings grief," you are saying yes to evolution. You are making a choice not only to be grateful for what you enjoy but to live in joy with circumstances that don't adhere to your preferences so that you can be evolved by them.

Develop Mental Flexibility. When experiencing something that is not your favorite, ask yourself, "What is the invitation here?" Stay with the question. Consider what would happen if you said, "Yes. I am willing . . ." A few years ago, my four grown sons suggested that we forgo our traditional Easter weekend for something different. No elaborate meal, no Easter baskets or egg hunt, and maybe a day for them to do something they really enjoyed. My response was an emphatic "No way!" I was attached to our Easter tradition and resisted their suggestion fiercely. I even played the guilt card: "Don't do this to your mother!" But at the suggestion of my husband, I also tried to imagine the reality they had suggested. What if I just said "yes" and tried that on for size before so quickly rejecting it with a reactive "no"? The day with my boys wouldn't require me to exhaust myself preparing for an elaborate celebration important mostly to me. A lovely catered meal would create minimal mess. I'd save the time and money normally spent on shopping for elaborate gifts for Easter baskets. On Sunday, the boys could do something they really wanted to do—go snowboarding and have some brother time. I could chill, rest, and read, things I love. When confronted with something that doesn't feel like a preference and a solid no starts to form in your mind, consider for a moment what would happen if you just said "yes."

Sometimes saying "yes" is accepting the unpreferred reality as if you chose it yourself. Getting fired from a job you didn't like anyway can become an opportunity to regroup, nurture yourself, and find work you do like. A pandemic delivers three months at the beach. A celebration can be different but equally satisfying. Try adding the word "fortunately" at the beginning of the thing you are resisting. "Fortunately, this is happening be-cause . . ." Exercises like this can diminish resistance and foster that welcoming heart.

Stay Curious. Resist the urge to label something too soon. Good? Bad? Who knows? Suspend judgment, stay in the space of not knowing, even if it's uncomfortable. Judgment attaches you to something in the short term, but beginner's mind helps you explore many perspectives and welcome whatever might be in store. It takes you off of the exhausting emotional roller coaster instigated by the ego's play-by-play of judging, naming, labeling, and suffering. Naming something puts you in the victim role, limits possibilities, and removes you from co-creating life.

Have Faith. Land on what is true for you. Do you believe that God has your back? Can you acknowledge that the universe is acting in your favor? Don't dismiss this. It's a big deal. Albert Einstein viewed the answers to these questions as foundational, the only way you could successfully move on. He proved that, at minimum, the universe is benevolent. No evil force is out to get you. It isn't personal, it isn't negative, it just is. Making a decision about faith isn't the end of the discussion, but it allows for hope. Be curious about how it might all turn out.

ANYTHING BUT GRATITUDE IS JUST A TANTRUM

By evolving my gratitude practice, going deeper, I realized that saying anything but "Thank you for what is all of my life" is the ego throwing a fit. It's a more subtle form of venting about what I don't like or approve of.

I immediately loved Anne Lamott's idea that we really need only three prayers: Help, Wow, and Thanks. But maybe it can be even simpler. "Help" is acknowledging a struggle and desire for assistance, but it's also an expression of disapproval with what's been presented to you and a lack of belief in what you are capable of. "Wow," that feeling of awe and wonder, basically sums up my beginning gratitude practice, the inventory of what I enjoyed or approved of.

By evolving my gratitude practice, I think I've boiled it down: "Thank you." This is what it sounds like in my life:

Thank you—I welcome it.

Thank you—I say yes to it.

Thanks—I maintain perspective.

Thanks—I remain curious.

Thanks—I am open to being evolved by it.

Thank you—I will sit in the mystery, with faith that God is good.

For me, the end game of my practice is to live effortlessly and organically, to be happy regardless of the daily unveilings. I want to dance with impermanence and hold fast to my belief that the universe has my back while being pretty sure it will all work out in the end or it's not the end.

That's why the only prayer I need is "Thank you. For all of it."

MOVING TO GRATITUDE 2.0

If you are unable to count everything as a blessing, to answer "Thank You" for all that happens, consider taking your practice to the next level. Keep a diary that accounts for the events and highlights of your day or week. Capture not just the experiences that made you feel good but all the moments that caught your awareness, big and small. What stood out for you? The goal is to create a more complete list, to evolve the practice so you can see everything as a blessing. See if you can find yourself able to welcome it all—with awe and excitement, willing to be shaped by the moment and willing to shape what's next out of your highest self.

1. Review the list and highlight, or put a star by, the things that are easy to greet with thanks. This is like the old practice, except you will have leftovers for comparison and contemplation.

2. Examine the unstarred remains. Work the gap—this is where your growth is.

3. Reflect on duality. Can you get rid of story, personal preferences, judgment, and attachment? What on the list feels especially intense? Try to transcend and realize the wholeness and the complexity of it.

4. Stay curious. Resist the urge to name or label something. That's judgment. Get neutral, develop a beginner's mind. Ask yourself, "How would I know?"

5. Tune into impermanence. Where are you resisting? What is your fear? (My Easter story is an example.) Actively work to stay in the present moment and grieve, then let go, remove resistance. Move forward with right action— kindness, compassion, new vision—from a place of acceptance.

6. Mine the experience for opportunity. How can you allow yourself to be evolved by what you're facing that feels frightening or unwanted? Will you be the prisoner or the monk?

7. Find your faith. If the universe is kind, or at least benevolent as Einstein found, commit to that belief. Don't trade what you know for sure for what you don't know. It bears repeating: "It's all okay in the end or it's not the end."

ENOUGH IS ENOUGH

On a long-ago retreat, I was invited to "walk with a word" for the day to open up to something that I needed or desired or to set an intention for how I wanted to be in the world. Choosing a word to focus on would be like a small light, blinking to remind me of the direction I wanted to go and the choices I could make to live the intention. Incorporating this simple practice into my life was significant.

I feel continual awe at the power of language, especially the way a single word can shape the way I see things.

Words help me subtly shift energy to delineate micro-boundaries. For example, when people come at me with negativity I don't want to participate in, I use neutral language like "Wow, that's good to know" to redirect the conversation. I say things like "I love that guy/woman" when others gossip about people I care about. That veers the conversation to something more productive, and I add, "What should we be doing to help?"

Consider the difference in language between "We just got

more work dumped on us" and "We've been assigned an important new project." Do you feel the difference?

Do you go to war with cancer or dance with it?

Sometimes words are given to me by a guru or teachers, like a mantra. Sometimes words find me. They crop up again and again, becoming an earworm, the sound of the cosmos tattooing something important into my consciousness. I pay attention to the words that keep showing up in my life, because I've come to know they are there to inspire me to think more deeply or to try on a new way of being.

Sometimes a single, simple word finds me, appearing forcefully. Other times, it flits into view, disappearing and reappearing like a colorful butterfly on a hiking trail, to teach me a lesson I didn't even realize I needed to learn. These are the words that influence, even redirect, my life perspective. I know I need to attend to them. Such words become my teachers.

One of those words recently adopted me and refused to leave my side: Enough.

Liberation resides in that simple, two-syllable word, which materialized again and again during a time of personal and professional uncertainty and trepidation. It assisted me in reframing my business goals. I used the word to ease the mind of loved ones who had become new parents. "Enough" fine-tuned my definition of love. "Enough" helped me end a great argument I was having with reality and articulate a regret I hadn't been able to name.

After the pandemic hit in the spring of 2020, I found utility in "enough." It helped me discard a way of being that wouldn't serve my current reality. Normally, my aspirations and the messages to my business team have been about growth. Let's get on bigger stages, find new audiences, amplify our message while maintaining a small footprint. Let's be No. 1 in our business! We focused on the metrics of more.

And because that was the way I had encouraged my team members to think, that was the mindset they brought when we talked about the COVID crisis. It had upended the world, including us, as our traditional offerings were either canceled or put on hold. The team wanted to react quickly, and our first conversations were understandably centered on finding different ways to continue growing and stay competitive. We talked about creating fresh offers, unconventional ways to make sales. The instinctive questions we wrestled with were, "How do we capitalize and take advantage of this opportunity? How do we not miss a beat?"

But as we talked, I started to feel a little hesitant. The conversation began to sound a bit tone-deaf. The world was falling apart. Maybe a big pivot and reinvention wasn't what we were being called to do. Maybe this wasn't a time to rev up but to slow down, to listen, and to reflect.

I realized the most important thing to me in these chaotic times was to make sure my team and my clients came through the time of COVID-19 safely and well. For that, maybe we needed more caring instead of more sales. It was like being in a car accident with your family on the way to a big event. The primary concern shouldn't be about whether you can get to the event on time. It should be: "Is everyone all right?"

I was a little shocked the first time I used the word "enough" on a business call. Maybe that was all we needed to weather the storm that was rocking our boat. I told my team, "Let's think about sitting tight and regrouping. Bottom line, let's focus on the minimum amount we need to bring in to make sure we have enough to get us through this." The word "enough" shifted our perspective in a way that created a sense of calm and security. We might have been knocked off our feet, but we didn't need to jump right up and charge ahead to make sure we didn't lose the race. We could sit and reflect a bit, be extra mindful as we made decisions about moving forward.

As I navigated this major disruption to my business income, it dawned on me that even though we had lost a lot, I have *enough* to live. I didn't want to be ruled by my business or the erratic cycles of the economy. Rather, I wanted to focus on the life I want and how I want to feel about my life. "Enough" sparked a recognition that I was provided for. All was provided for. I longed for nothing. My new life goal was to remember that I had enough, and that I was enough.

But the word wasn't done with me yet.

A few months later the word reappeared as my colleagues Alex and Ana were going through a difficult stretch in their roles as new parents. They'd had their first baby, a beautiful son, and had adapted to parenthood beautifully. As with all new parents, they were focused on doing it right, being the perfect caregivers for their precious firstborn infant. When the baby started having a hard time getting enough to eat, I could see and feel how stressful it was for them. They were getting plenty of advice, and I didn't want to add to their stress with more. Even so, I wanted to support them, help in any way I could. On one of my daily walks, I tuned into a podcast that had advertised an interview with one of my favorite authors. I felt a little irritated to discover he wouldn't be talking about his work but rather his top three favorite books. But I kept listening, and eventually he mentioned a book I'd been introduced to during my education in psychology in the 1980s: *A Good Enough Parent.*

Enough! That word again. I couldn't wait to share what I'd heard with Alex and Ana. Maybe a slight lowering of expectations could ease the burden of overwhelming responsibility they were feeling. Perfect parenting is impossible, and they were good enough parents. The word "enough" seemed to settle them and bolster their confidence.

This recurring visitor was satisfying to greet when it appeared. I began to embrace "enough" and to walk with it more frequently. I opened up to this word, felt curious about it, not as a means of achieving mastery but of honoring mystery. I wanted to let it guide me, to follow it instead of trying to figure it out.

In contemplation of all the meanings of "enough," I realized how many areas of my life the word applied to. How can "enough" spark anything but gratitude? The word quells my restless desire for more. What if we all felt assured that we had enough and that we are enough? The word began to reshape the way I viewed my relationships, including one I lost and another I knew I soon would lose.

After my friend Cathy's cancer diagnosis, we made a plan and commitments to each other. I promised to accompany her to the furthest edge possible as she passed. We had no expectations about when death would arrive or exactly how it would take her, but when the time came, I made the commitment to be with her, near her, and completely available.

After one particularly meaningful conversation with Cathy, I was speaking to another mutual friend, Pam, about the existential themes Cathy and I had discussed. Pam exclaimed, "Damn, girl! You have courage!"

Over the years, many people have told me I am brave, that I have great courage. I have considered it a compliment, a verbal recognition of a moral characteristic that had been baked into my personality. It felt like something I could claim—I had cultivated courage. I owned it! Why did Pam's use of the word that day leave me so unsettled? The fact that it did started me thinking more deeply about the word "courage."

My commitment to be fully present with Cathy as she died might have appeared courageous, but in truth, it wasn't. It was rooted in something else, just like my courage to speak from a stage before thousands of people wasn't about bravery but my unwillingness to disappoint the people who had booked me or who had come to hear me speak. Sometimes I stayed in relationships that didn't work because I didn't have the courage to leave. Like those things, what I was doing with Cathy didn't seem connected to courage, it was more about my fear of living without her.

A few days after my conversations with Cathy and Pam, I was on the phone with a matchmaker. I wasn't up for the online dating scene, but someone had introduced me to a local matchmaker. I was hoping she could introduce me to a few interesting guys who, in the time of COVID, would be game for conversations on Zoom. It's the ultimate safe dating setup for introverts, right?

As a way of determining what I was looking for, she asked me to identify a fulfilling relationship, one in which I felt well-loved.

I started a list of relationship hopes:

Unconditional support.

An ability to be present while I struggled without the need to fix or control.

Someone who took a long perspective, was patient.

A person who trusted me and my process.

Someone who would be a soft place to land when I made mistakes or the world kicked my ass.

Someone who truly saw me and loved exactly what they saw.

"Basically, someone just like my Cathy Frost, only better in bed," I joked. "I want the male version of her."

Cathy had, for more than thirty years, been my true love. She was the ideal, a brilliant example of what I was looking for in a relationship. What was it about her love that had been so amazing? Once again, the word "enough" sat on my shoulder. Cathy, in all my ups and downs, through prosperity and scarcity, always saw me as whole—enough.

She was there to insist I could push that baby out. Cathy nurtured me through divorces and deaths. When I confessed to going on another date with someone I didn't even like, she didn't judge or advise. She simply said, "It sounds like you needed more research." She was supportive when I found new love and stood by me when it began to fall apart. She held my hand through boom-and-bust business ventures. When I was dealing with family tragedies, she was the first person to show up, steadfast in her total acceptance of me. She never made me feel like I was anything other than enough.

For me, Cathy has defined what it is to be "well-loved"—that utter knowing that I was always enough.

That's why Pam's use of the word "courageous" seemed coun-
terfeit. Being with Cathy when she left her body wasn't about
courage, it was an attempt to delay the terrifying moment when
I would have to live in a world without her in it. And while
people used the word "courageous" to describe Cathy's commitment to facing death with grit and grace, I also knew, because
she had told me, she was wrestling with her own fears. When
she confessed her desire to be cremated along with a strong un-
dercurrent of irrational fear about being burned, I promised to
be in the vicinity of where it would happen, to lend my energy.
It calmed her. What was happening with Cathy and me wasn't
about an individual, heroic effort of vanquishing fear. Whatever
courage I had was tied directly to her. I could be there for her
because of who she was to me and how she had shaped my life. I
could do these really hard things not because I was so brave but
because I was so well loved.

I could take risks—in business, in love, in parenting, in life—
with rock-solid knowledge that Cathy's love for me was constant
and never-ending, no matter how things turned out. When I did
"dumb" things or made less-than-stellar choices, her attitude
was that I was experiencing everything as I should and at just
the right time.

What a gift to know that someone will always be there for
you. They witness the hits and the misses, the mistakes and the
miracles, with unshakeable faith and knowledge that you are all
you need to be. With every conversation and act of friendship,
they telegraph that you are enough.

Throughout Cathy's and my last days together, the word
"enough" continued to visit. It became a way to help quell our

doubt and regrets, to avoid suffering when it began to beckon. On the rare occasions that Cathy would talk about our unfulfilled plans, the bucket list items that would never come to fruition, I could say: "Cathy, we've had just enough fun." When we recalled the painful times we had experienced together, times when we screamed about pain and injustice and cursed the universe, she would remind me in return: "We've had just enough heartbreak." When she apologized for not calling me back for a week because she'd been too exhausted to talk, I would say: "This week has really tired you out. Just know that however you need to get through the day is enough. It's enough. You have been there for me enough, and you are enough.

"Know that I love you so much, and I know you love me. I grew up, from my twenties to my fifties, being absolutely convinced that you loved me. That I was enough. That's what gave me, what gives me, courage to do hard stuff. We still have hard stuff to do, but I'm in it fully.

"We've had enough time together. We have enough time left to let go."

As I continued reflecting, I let the word "enough" actively unravel me and redefine how I viewed love itself. Had I done for others what Cathy did for me? For my kids? If love was being present in a way that people knew, right down to the marrow in their bones, that they were enough, how had I done?

Well, certainly I could have done better, and I could do better. I could use every moment of time with my grown sons to affirm they are *enough* as they are right now in the world as it is. I could let go of trying to influence their decisions or suggest ways they should improve their lives. They have plenty of time to figure things out. I don't need to direct my twenty-four-year-old son on how he should vote or insist that my boys and I spend every holiday embedded in tradition. Unsolicited help is about control, my ego trying to arrange the world as I want and need it to be. I would work to be better, to love people up to my new standard, "You are enough."

Even as I felt a fresh sort of bliss for having defined and committed to love on a different level, I turned to my grief over the loss of a love—the man I had recently divorced. My contemplation turned to my contributions to a relationship that didn't work. I was curious about whether I had loved my husband in that way. When I asked that question, I had a sinking feeling that maybe I hadn't. And when I looked more deeply, I realized I'd been so worried that maybe I wasn't enough for him that I directed my efforts into creating something great for us.

From my perspective, I did so much for him, elevated him in my world as the one person to please and to cherish, and forgave him so much. During our marriage, I worked hard, I dug deep, I did therapy, I reframed, I practiced all I knew about what I thought love was. I exhausted myself trying to create a great life for us. And doing that seemed to require brushing aside issues of equity and mutual support that were essential to me.

Love can be unconditional, but relationships need conditions. To stay in the marriage, I knew I needed certain things. I could ask for what I need, listen intently to the response and respect it as his truth, and then stay or go. Over several years, I extended the invitation for him to meet me there, and he consistently declined. I kept arguing with that reality until eventually I achieved clarity. For my own integrity, I needed to say: "Enough is enough"—not in a threatening way but to make it bright and clear what my boundaries were.

My hope was that "enough is enough" would allow us to come together in a different way, but it didn't work out like that.

In the wake of ending that relationship, "enough" appeared to me as an articulation of a regret I hadn't been able to express or shake off as I reflected on the complexities of our marriage and the pain of ending it. I still remember his reaction to the news that I wanted a divorce. And I wonder—I worry—whether he heard that *he* wasn't enough instead of that what *we were creating together* was insufficient.

My message got muddled. My regret is not making it clear that he is enough whether we were together or not. For that, I am so sorry. Today I would love to have him know—to have everyone I love in my life know—that they are enough. Don't believe anything that makes you feel otherwise.

Words are so powerful. Listen, be curious and attentive to the words that appear and sometimes come to stay.

"Enough" changed my perspective and cracked open my heart. Now I see a role for myself in easing suffering in the world by easing the shame that happens when we take in the message that we are not enough.

You are enough, we were enough, we had enough. Our time together was enough. The time we have left is enough. I have always had enough. There will always be enough.

This word hasn't gone away—it keeps hanging around. You might want to let that word take hold of you, too.

THE POWER OF "AND"

Walking with a special word (whether I choose it or it chooses me) gives me a guiding virtue and helps me stay focused on the ways I want to show up in the world. One word I always keep close is a mundane, utilitarian conjunction that keeps me out of the illusion of limitations, helps me transcend the trap of duality, and opts me out of polarity's tug-of-war.

I love the little word "and."

These three simple letters strung together are a superpower. Liberation from polarity, poor choices, and victimhood is found in the word "and." This little word eliminates helplessness, expands your mind, and opens the heart. It connotes endless possibility, which sparks creativity and fuels innovation. It's the quickest possible fix to the stickiest of dilemmas, providing instant reframes and fast relief from judgment and suffering.

"And" can be represented by a singular symbol—an ampersand, a plus sign. Yet like a single cell, it can grow into something large, complex, and beautiful, this word is much more than adding one thing to another. "And" doesn't just acknowledge two or more different sides, it instantly elevates thinking. It allows me to see beyond the tree into the forest, the mountains, the sky, and the universe. "And" helps me transcend the pain inherent in duality; it gives permission to acknowledge paradox and plot twists. It shows me the way to do hard things.

Wow. Who wouldn't want to keep this singular, super-charged word at the ready?

MANY THINGS CAN BE TRUE AT THE SAME TIME

Understanding the multiple ways that seemingly contradictory things can be true at once is one of the keys to contentment. Using "and" is a way to remove the self-imposed blinders of a narrowed view. If you can sit with this concept, really meditate on it, you'll find rapid access to compassion and develop a higher tolerance for the world's messiness.

The mind, which evolved to emphasize survival, tends to default to an "either/or" perspective, which shuts down possibilities and limits the fullness of life. Yet we choose this perspective again and again. Why? Because the ego loves safety and certainty and chooses those qualities over accuracy—and definitely over complexity.

Thinking in absolutes is the mind's common, natural response to the stress of complexity. In our early days as humans, thinking in absolutes drove survival. As a nomadic, prehistoric human, if I needed water, I wanted to know if water was in the watering hole a mile away. A simple, clear answer would be helpful in deciding whether to use my limited energy to go there or in a different direction.

But let's say I ask a complex thinker that question: Is there water in the hole? She says yes. I ask her again, "Is there NO water in the hole?" And she says yes. WHAT? The complex reality is that there is both water and not water in the hole (some elements are non-water, and some are water). It's closer to the truth but not helpful in that moment of survival. I want a simple answer. Either there is water in the hole *or* there is no water. Not having a single, clear answer creates stress and an uncomfortable condition known as cognitive dissonance.

The primitive "either/or" solution to cognitive dissonance is an obstacle to connecting, meaning, and wholehearted living—the very things we crave. To live fully in the mess, we need to become skilled at paradoxical thinking and develop the ability to hold space for multiple things to be true at the same time. We need to learn to get comfortable with the uneasiness caused by cognitive dissonance, which appeals to our survival instinct and puts the ego on red alert. With practice, we can thwart the ego's goal to feel better by overriding the "either/or" thinking habit.

Trying to force this beautiful, complex world into the prison of a two-dimensional, diametric space will inevitably lead to long-term suffering. When we evolve to live with the discomfort cognitive dissonance can create, infinite possibilities appear. That's why I love "and." It helps relieve the stress of cognitive dissonance and allows for a richer experience.

As a therapist, I was trained in an approach called Dialectical Behavior Therapy, a method that teaches people to live in the moment, to regulate emotion, and to develop and maintain healthy relationships. One of the key concepts is helping people recognize, and live successfully in, a world where many things are true at the same time. For instance, it's possible to care deeply about someone and be furious with them—at the same time. For a person who feels so miserable they want to die, and yet they also want to live, the choice can seem tortuous: either misery or death. What if there were another choice—to create a less painful life that fuels the desire to live?

Yet people want to cling to duality. We can't have this AND that because they are contradictory. It starts when we're young. How often do we ask children what they want to be when they grow up, with the underlying assumption that they can only be one thing? We've been almost brainwashed into believing that we have to choose between financial abundance through laser focus, hustle, and 24/7 devotion to career OR choose healthy relationships, creativity, and purpose while sacrificing wealth. What kind of choice is that? A false one.

The foundation of my success is the work I've done to integrate my ability to see the world differently, to creatively write about it with great stories, and to combine that with business savvy. I am a creator and a maker and a writer and a business advisor and a successful CEO, among other things.

I've been asked so many times: "How do you work and raise four boys?" The implication is that if I am dedicated to both, either my work or my sons are suffering. But I can transcend that limited choice with a different question: How do I create and enjoy success in my business and create and enjoy experiences with my sons—at the same time? When the question includes "and," create and enjoy are on both sides of the conjunction.

My focus expands to creation and enjoying the whole of my life rather than accepting that one part takes away from the other.

Your potential, your possibilities, and your satisfying answers are rarely going to be on either side of "or." When confronted with mess, the tendency is to think that one choice is right, the other wrong. We need either this OR that. You're with me OR against me. We can win OR lose.

The "or" problem troubled me as I made plans for the last half of my life. I was feeling stressed because I couldn't clearly define that "magic number" of resources required for me to stop working so hard and start playing. I fretted I'd get the number and the timing wrong. How many times have you heard stories about someone finally retiring and then having health issues that prevented them from fully enjoying it? I saw only polarity—either I could work the crazed schedule of a business owner or I could retire with nagging worries about living on a fixed income.

What a sucker's choice!

"And" came to the rescue. I reframed the question: How might I adjust my life to continue activities that bring desired income AND find ways to create and enjoy more free time?

Whoa. Thinking beyond duality allowed me to see choices beyond "running a fast-paced, all-consuming business" or "not running such a business." What if I rebalanced work and play as it fit my energy and desires AND kept my options open through networking and wise investing?

"And" allows me to live in the mystery. I'm not being boxed in by a rigid, long-term plan. When you refuse to be imprisoned by a limited view of the world that divides things into Either/Or, and the human race into Us/Them, that is freedom.

Start listening for the times you begin to use dangerous phrases like "I know . . ." or "We only have . . ." or "We must choose . . ." When you hear those words, you've devolved into primitive thinking and a limited view.

"And" is a wonderful tool for subverting the ego's instinct to armor up and keep us from seeing the sweet abundance of nearly infinite options. With vigilance and practice, "and" helps you develop enough mental flexibility to crack that armor. As Leonard Cohen says, the cracks show where the light is.

OPEN HEARTS AND MINDS

Another way we get boxed in is by insisting on simplicity when it comes to emotion. And what can feel messier than emotions? "And" gives us permission to "feel all our feels," with a nod to the web of complex and seemingly contradictory emotions we often experience at the same time. All are worth honoring.

In the last year or so, I've been starting meetings and conversations with folks by asking them to name two things they're feeling in the moment. The expansiveness of the answers I hear has been illuminating. I hear things like, "I'm feeling anxious about the future and also excited about what's possible." One person said she was feeling both "shattered and delighted"—shattered because a dear friend had received a hard health diagnosis and delighted because her daughter was accepted into a program she'd worked hard to get into. I heard the response "angry and grateful." This person was angry about some of the blatant racism that was happening in this country and grateful that it had been seen and had spurred people to action. You can be excited about holidays and feel sad because they remind you of loved ones no longer there to celebrate.

This allowance for experiencing and embracing many emotions at the same time makes space for creativity and signals an openness to new ideas. When people open their hearts, their minds often expand as well.

HEART OPENING

The ability to integrate many emotions at the same time opens you up to a multidimensional life where your whole reality isn't defined by a single feeling. When you realize that emotions come rapidly and eventually ebb, you don't have to be afraid to feel them in the moment.

I saw this up close after my niece lost her fifteen-year-old son in a terrible car accident. Grief wound around her in a deep and profound way. How could she ever enjoy her life again when her son had been robbed of his?

And yet, happiness wanted to assert itself from time to time. One weekend she was at my house for an extra dose of solace and support. I saw her smile as she watched young neighbor boys fishing and playing on the beach. In that moment, her grief was swept away, and she was momentarily caught up in a feeling she hadn't experienced for a while—joy. But then guilt bumped up against her vigilant, singular identity as a grieving mom. If she was happy in the moment, it must mean she didn't miss her son, didn't mourn his loss.

Her son, Drew, had loved being at the lake. He'd had so much fun fishing from our dock and had even taught some of those same little boys how to do it. When my niece caught herself experiencing a moment of happiness, her instinctual response was to evict joy. As she reminded herself that Drew was gone, she descended into suffering. Anger, sadness, and heartbreak seemed like the only acceptable emotions. She was invited by this experience to see that a moment of joy didn't require her to stop missing her son or to desist in her grief. The ego was trying to force a false choice—grief or joy. If she could embrace "and," she could integrate both emotions and have the full dimension of her life experience. Feeling joy could be part of remembering and honoring Drew. Grief and joy, peacefully co-existing.

It's a trap to think we can only feel one emotion at a time, and it can lead to faulty decisions. If I miss my former husband, does that mean I made a mistake in leaving? If I'm feeling joy and relief in the wake of a painful divorce, does it mean that I didn't love him? Of course not. I can miss him, love him, AND recognize it was the right decision for me to leave. Feelings aren't right or wrong. They're just . . . feelings. Catch them and release them. It's not only okay to have many different feelings, it's absolutely natural. It's human. "And" helps you recognize that.

"AND" FOSTERS SELF-ACCEPTANCE

The word "and" also is useful for depersonalizing feedback. Just because someone has given you data about how you're perceived in the world, it doesn't have to define who you are. Humans are complex, multifaceted beings—sometimes we're kind, and sometimes we're cruel. You can be great at money management and also capable of careless spending. You can be a loving parent and find yourself snapping at the kids.

By remembering that the feedback doesn't define who you are, it's easier to scale back on defensiveness. Maybe you can make space for the possibility that data you've been given is real, residing among your virtues and your shadows. Relating to information in this way can increase self-compassion and acceptance.

While growing up, I sometimes would be upset about something someone said to me that I perceived as mean and hurtful. When I'd tell my mom about it, the injustice of it all, she'd say something like, "Oh, sweetheart, I want you to know that in my book, you are absolutely perfect. AND you could stand some improvement."

Often, when presented with new information we don't want to believe, our instinct is to double down on what we think we know. If I *know* I am perfect, then I don't need to consider that, just maybe, I could use some improvement.

My mom's use of the word "and" helped me expand the view and consider the fact that I wasn't just "one thing." My identity was not fixed. And notice she didn't use the word "but," the word that we wield like a sword to defend ourselves. "I might not be perfect, but I'm not what you say I am."

"And" helps resolve the false conflict: I am perfect as I am. And I am imperfect. I am a good person. And I could be better.

When you're feeling on the ropes, try swapping "but" with "and." Feel the shift.

I messed up, ~~but~~ and I can try to make it up.

I am disappointed about your choice, ~~but~~ and I love you.

I understand your point, ~~but~~ and I have a different perspective than you do.

I am doing my best, ~~but~~ and I can try harder.

"And" is a way to create a fuller, more authentic view of ourselves and others. It becomes less necessary to strive to be more kind—you become more kind. Using "and" can instantly open your heart to compassion and help you to see people in a new light. Next time you find yourself irritated with someone, or assigning them a label, try on the word "and." It immediately widens your perspective.

"His car is always so messy! AND he works really long hours. AND he hasn't had much time to get a good organizing system in place. AND a messy car might not bother him." In the space of a few sentences, "and" can move you from judging someone as a messy pig to having compassion for a busy guy who is doing the best he can.

You might not ever know the truth of it, but you can't even consider possibilities if you are unwilling to see them. The world instantly grows more kind if we can become compassionately willing for it all to be true.

CREATE SAFETY WHILE CALLING OTHERS TO GREATNESS

The word "and" can help people talk about tough topics and ultimately do hard things together. It's one of the ways I have learned to create safety for others while calling them up to greatness. "And" helps you stay in relationship with someone as you co-create a better future. It makes room for the human condition of growing and evolving and yes, even regressing at times.

"And" is a way to reassure and request something different. Its use keeps compassion as a foundation in conversations that call out behavior that might be undesirable or in need of changing without calling into question that someone is human and lovable.

Remembering "and" opens up my heart when I need to have tough conversations. It helps me come with a loving heart and create psychological safety as we conjure up different, bigger, and better things for the future. Using "and" alerts them that I recognize that they are not their behavior.

"I love you, and I'd like to see your behavior change."

"I love you, and I need to know if you're willing to focus on this issue with me."

"I care about you, and I'm asking you to be on time or to call when you're going to be late."

EXPANDING YOUR THINKING

If a dilemma is viewed in polarity or mutual exclusivity, innovation is killed, scarcity is invoked, and hope for inventive solutions is lost. Which side are you on? Which camp are you in?

Who decided the world was divided into two camps? I believe in one camp—the human camp. I want to be on the side that takes into account everyone and the planet. The world is abundant. The ego would like you to think otherwise, and it shows up big and bold in challenging times that require problem solving.

Sometimes in meetings with my staff, I respond to a seemingly tough choice between two unpreferred options with the question "Where's the 'and' here?"

When I hear "or" creeping into the conversation, I know we're framing potential solutions from a place of fear. "Do we grow the business or keep the status quo?" "Do we go all in or wait for a return to normal?" "Do we find ways to increase profits or ways to protect the environment?" With "or," not only are solutions more obscure, you've likely framed two equally bad choices.

We had a major breakthrough this year as we tried to figure out whether or not to give up our office space. We were tied to an office in a city that no longer excited most of the staff, including me, and the virus had us temporarily working at home. Should we set up to work from home permanently or renew the office lease? By continuously asking where the "and" would lead us, we broke through. The dreaming and scheming began. Why be limited to one of two unpreferred options? We could set up "mini spaces" to work anywhere our hearts desired! We moved beyond the notion of a set studio and found ways to do great virtual work wherever we were. We found a software system that allows fluent communication about clients no matter who was in the record. Asking "Where is the 'and' in this situation?" allowed us to free ourselves up from relying on a small geographical area from which to draw top talent.

"And" also can be an antidote to something I call "bundling." When I find myself reluctant to consider the innovative or big ideas of others, I try to self-reflect about what fuels my resistance. It's usually bundling.

To preemptively build a case for the status quo, my ego bundles my support of an idea with the burden of having to do all the work to make it successful. If I say "yes," my ego works to make me believe the illusion that I am agreeing to make it happen. I have more than enough on my plate, so "no" seems like a safer response.

"And" to the rescue. I combine "yes" plus "and," which opens me to possibilities without feeling like I have to take them all on. I can offer acceptance and support without scope creep. "Yes and" means I can support, align with, and encourage something without the burden of owning it. It's another call to greatness. "Yes, I support you in this, and now I am willing to help you think through how you could make that happen." We can dream together expansively without the worry that it will be my responsibility to make your dream come true.

Like everything, "and" can be tricky. It can be used to cast a shadow that creates a hiding place for subtle, unspoken conditions. "How can I be honest and not have you be mad at me?" You want to be honest (the desire), and you want to control the other's reaction to your honesty (the condition). Your choice to be honest is yours. Another person's emotional reaction to your honesty is theirs. While you can work to share honestly and respectfully, you can't ever guarantee or manage their reaction. By using "and" in such a situation, you signal a condition on the willingness to live your values: I will be honest only if I know that there isn't any risk.

A better use of "and" in that case is "I choose to be honest and kind *and* I am willing to say this knowing that it could be difficult for you to hear."

In today's world, my superpower word has never been more important. "And" is code for "I am pretty sure I don't know everything." I might not be able to have it all, but I can embrace everything as true and possible. Cognitive dissonance doesn't have to shrink the possibilities. It can usher in a greater tolerance for living in the mess.

Knowing and accepting that many things are true at the same time makes living in the mess a lot more peaceful. If you allow "and" to roll up its sleeve and get to work, this sweet little word will usher in an evolved and expansive perspective of the world.

GIVEN

Let's face it, times get super tough. Life gets messy. The year 2020, when I was writing this book, was one of the messiest of my life. When obstacles appear and crises arise, it's tempting to let circumstances become the reason I can't create the life I want to have. "This is what I want, but the details of these messy circumstances are blocking me from my desires and all progress."

"Given" is one of my favorite words to initiate a pivot. I have come to cherish this word because it can quickly get me unstuck when faced with disruptions to my nicely laid out plans. It allows me to adjust to unexpected setbacks from a difficult or complicated reality. When reality dishes out challenges that initially look like brick walls, "given" reminds me that my circumstances don't have to determine my behavior. I can still achieve my goals by choosing the best action in the reality in which I find myself. When I am mired in the constraints that a difficult reality presents, I use "given" to help me to step into the power I have. It's a doorway to the space in which I can have an impact. It shifts the energy from "I can't" to "How could I?"

"Given" begins a statement, which leads to a good question, which shows me I have choices to move forward: "Given that others are panicked by the loss of work, how can I remain calm and grounded?" "Given that this pandemic has radically changed the demand for our current offerings, how can we adapt and create offerings that are relevant to today and valuable enough to restore revenue?"

Living in the mess means we'll often confront what I call an "unpreferred" reality. When faced with an unpreferred reality, we overfocus on what we wish were different about the current state. We plow energy into defining, imagining, and fantasizing about how we would like things to be easier and less disruptive. But seriously, what power do we have to change the right now? While we rail against reality with fruitless arguments, reality folds its arms, leans back, and says, "This is what is. Period." You will lose any and all arguments with reality, but only 100 percent of the time.

The arguments will not only exhaust you, they'll also blind you to the power you have to co-create a different, more desired future. Arguing with reality robs you of the opportunity to be your best self *in the moment*. And just hoping things will get better can't affect the future.

But there is a small space between an unpreferred reality and a preferred future where we can build a bridge. Actions in response to the moment can help co-create the future.

Your power resides in radically accepting what is, stopping the arguments, and resisting the urge to succumb to reality as if it were the only determinant of your future. Reality stops being an excuse for lack of action and becomes just one of the elements of current circumstances.

Creating questions using "given" reframes what I see as obstacles into simply new information. My perspective shifts from seeing only what stands in the way to a view of the possibilities within reality's frame.

Instead of passively accepting our lot in life, "given" encourages us to identify potential. It shows actions we can take right now, or the alternate ways we can be, that will impact the way we are experiencing the now. We get connected to a different next.

"Given" greets reality with neutrality, free of story, and provides an antidote to suffering. It transmutes the details of reality's exceptional, powerful obstacles to a neutral view of how it is and what is possible in the midst of it. While the word "and" typically leads to bigger thinking overall, the word "given" locates the space in which to maneuver the escape hatch. We often want to dream and scheme and think big, but sometimes constructing a smaller, compact container for what can actually be done *now* can get us unstuck.

When I hear people say "We can't, because this reality is stopping us," I use "given" to restore hope, foster innovation, and remind people they are not victims. Given that reality is often messy, how can we be happy or successful anyway?

I'm comfortable with asking for help in achieving goals. My experience is that people are usually willing, even eager, to get on board. And then I watch as their good intentions get thwarted when tricky challenges arise. "Ugh, I wanted to get that done, but that danged reality got in the way." They twirl in the whirlpool of a difficult reality and see no way out. They quickly default to the belief that new circumstances determine destiny. What happens next?

In those situations, we often lament how our lives are messy and getting messier. People recite all the good reasons reality has prevented progress, with bountiful excuses for inaction. In these moments, we resort to being soothed by good intentions even though we have few results.

When others let us down, many of us opt for understanding and sympathy. It's easy to do—our lives are crazy, too! We even help them come up with more excuses. We collude with the notion that reality is thwarting movement. We should let people off the hook. After all, we can relate—we've had a lot of good intentions, and we haven't always lived up to them. Sometimes we even take back the request or passively acquiesce to the messiness.

When this happens to me, weirdly enough, my ego loves it! I am apt to decide this means if I want something, I'll just have to do it myself. I'll show people how things get done! It reinforces my arrogant and old belief that "I have to do everything around here." If I am not careful, I can use it to fuel my narrow thinking—I should never ask for help again. My ego constructs the case for superiority, victimhood, martyrdom, and, of course, suffering, which adds layers to the disappointment of my reality. My limiting beliefs get reinforced.

That's when it's time to pull out my secret weapon. It instantly ends the argument with the reality of the moment.

- Given that this person has not responded to your email after twenty-four hours, how can you get an answer by end of day?

- Given that I can't meet people in person or go out to the stores, how can I care for or be available to my neighbors?

- Given that information about the virus is changing and we can't know everything, what can you and I do today to keep ourselves as healthy and safe as possible?

- Given that we're short-staffed right now, how can I contribute more to make sure the essential work gets done?

- Given that others are not exhibiting their best behavior right now, how can I remain patient and kind?

What a helpful word! So subtle and yet so powerful. It doesn't preclude empathy, and it's not just a form of wishful or positive thinking. It's a call to expanded thinking, mental flexibility, and innovation. "Given" shifts the energy away from the barriers of "why we can't" to the innovations of "how we could." It puts a focus on hope and gives us a role in its comeback.

The word came in handy with clients I worked with during the pandemic. After a few weeks of working from home, some employees were informed they would need to return to their office building for a few days each pay period, even though the pandemic raged on. Many employees were panicked and angry. They began to point out the obstacles presented by the current reality that made the request unreasonable—even impossible. There were three hundred employees and not enough elevators to ensure social distancing without egregious waits. Some people worried about inadequate health and safety measures in the cafeteria. They wanted guarantees their employer had thought of everything so they would be safe from infection. They saw only "can't" in their options: "I can't go to work and risk illness or death by COVID. I can't say no and risk getting fired."

Those were daunting circumstances—no one was making stuff up. The reality was they were being required to resume work in an office environment as the pandemic continued. Elevator space was limited. The cafeteria remained open. Health and safety measures had been put in place, but they couldn't guarantee people wouldn't get the virus.

I had a lot of empathy for that challenging situation. And though I didn't have the solution, I could use "given" to help them reframe the situation and see possibilities.

"Given that you want to keep your job and are required to return to the office, how could you do it as safely as possible? Given that no one can guarantee you will remain healthy and have zero risk of infection, how could you make this work in the safest, most efficient way?"

As "given" shifted the energy, people began to see more possibilities. A few quickly realized they could take the stairs instead of the elevator. Many began to think of things that they could do, such as wear masks at work, wash their hands frequently, and carry hand sanitizer. Those concerned about food safety could bring lunch from home instead of eating in the cafeteria. Some could ask for a different shift to avoid the times the elevators were likely to be busiest. All soon realized that they could stop expecting their bosses to take full responsibility for their health and safety and share in the accountability. Rather than depending upon leaders to think of everything, they could lean in, point out risks not yet identified, and make suggestions as new things were discovered. Those first into the office could help colleagues by sharing tips and techniques they found helpful.

Even in the serious reality of a temporary situation that presented big obstacles, there were options. "Given" helped them find a way forward in spite of them.

So much energy goes into wishing circumstances were different that, at times, we are blind to the action that could have impact in this very moment, even if it's just being different. Wishful thinking can become the fuel that keeps you at the mercy of your story. Given things are a little messy, what action can be taken right now in spite of the mess? Maybe you can't overcome all things, but you can open up to possibilities for movement.

You can live in the mess (and there will always be a mess, by the way) by developing strategies and using tools that help you not become consumed by the elements of the mess. A word like "given" will help you quickly get to a reframe, to hold space, to take a small step, even if it is just to be kind anyway.

"Given" can help you acknowledge the realities that bump up against your resiliency. The word eliminates excuses and reminds you that reality is what you are called upon to impact. It will help you stay the course.

The fastest way to alter an unpreferred reality is to stop the argument with that reality and put energy into co-creating a different future. Stop letting reality manufacture excuses for staying stuck, and recognize you are simply facing the circumstances in which you must act. "Now" is what happens right before the future, and you have the power to connect the two. Given that life is always messy, "given" can keep you focused on what you can do to live happily in this moment and in these circumstances.

PART TWO

EVOLVE YOURSELF

HOLDING MY BREATH

I am a breath holder.

This is a fact, but symbolism also resides in the statement. My lifelong propensity to hold my breath gave birth to a metaphor, which sparked insights that are helping me manage my life in a more balanced and peaceful way.

I came by my breath-holding habit at a young age. As I was the sixth in a family of seven kids, my baby brother, Tim, and I were often assigned to one of our two oldest sisters for care. It's not that my parents weren't loving or attentive, but they had careers, responsibilities, and, well, five other kids.

Honestly, I was scared of both of my sisters back then. They were teenagers, pissed off about being shackled to these pesky miniature humans when they had their own lives to attend to. They used to argue in the morning about which of them would get who. Which of us would need the least effort as the day progressed? Who would be the least amount of trouble? Later, when we were adults, my sisters joked that the decision often came down to whose poopy diaper had been changed last. I learned at a young age that people were less likely to get mad at you—and to choose you—if you didn't exhibit too many needs or disturb their peace.

I learned to be the low-drama kid early in life, but my breath-holding habit was rooted in two high-drama events. One sprang from my sister's unwanted childcare duties. Sharri played on a softball team, and a few times a week, she had to haul me with her to practice. She would strap me into a kid's seat on the back of her bike, ride to the field, dismount, and put the kickstand down, leaving me in my seat. Her instructions were stern and clear: "If you move, the bike will fall over."

It was kind of like telling a kid, "Learn to meditate." Only, you know, I was four. (Who knows? Maybe that's where my ability to focus came from.) Anyway, I would hold my breath to keep from moving because I was really afraid of falling over.

One summer day we were at the ball park and I was dressed in the little halter top and shorts my sister Lorann had made me. Black clouds suddenly dominated the sky; the wind got gusty and fierce. Sharri and her teammates scattered as the weather changed, and she sprinted to the bike. We took off, trying to outrace the storm, which would not let us win. The rain was fierce, and to me, it was as if the softballs Sharri had recently been hitting had turned to ice and were pelting us from above. Her quick thinking saved the day as she pulled into the garage of one of my parents' rental properties to get us out of the weather.

We were both soaked and cold to the bone. I began to shiver uncontrollably. Shivering felt like something I shouldn't be doing, like my body was betraying me. I worried Sharri would get mad. I held my breath in an attempt to stop. Sharri noticed. "Oh, it's okay," she said to me, her kind tone surprising me. "You've got to breathe. It's okay to shiver. That's how you stay warm." And as I allowed myself a deep exhale, I remember my little brain thinking, "That's the nicest thing she's ever said to me." Her permission for me to have human tendencies made me feel loved. It was a huge bonding moment for us.

The other high-drama event had happened more than a year before, when I was only three. I don't remember much of it, but I have heard the stories so many times that the memories belong to me now, and they seem clear.

It began at Christmas. My brothers got sunflower seeds in their stockings, and, don't ask me how, I managed to aspirate one of them. It landed in my bronchial tube. Soon after, I developed a chronic cough and got really sick. After one coughing fit, the seedy culprit lodged in my trachea, cutting off my air supply. I choked—as in literally turning blue and passing out.

At the ER in my little town, the doctor urgently set about saving my life. With no time for anesthesia, my mom and others had to hold me down as Dr. Bennetti quickly made an incision in my throat to open my air passage. There was a lot of blood, and it was traumatic for everyone involved.

I became the town's big news story, the little girl who, deprived of air for a significant time, survived. The doctor became a hero. But no one realized the sunflower seed was still there, wedged between the trach tube and my trachea, where it would wreak additional havoc.

The story got more dramatic over the next several months as doctors tried to figure out my mystery "illness." The obvious diagnosis seemed to be whooping cough, which was raging in our community. The doctor prescribed penicillin, which caused a severe allergic reaction. The cough took a backseat to the urgent issue of skin peeling off my body.

As they dealt with that, I kept getting sicker. High fever. Issues with my lungs. At the time, X-rays were the only tool to see what was going on. On the X-ray slides, the little organic seed looked like mucus, not a foreign object lodged in my windpipe.

As my condition worsened, I was sent to the bigger regional hospital. Eventually I recovered enough to be discharged, so doctors pulled out my trach tube. We left the hospital and headed for a drive-in restaurant in my hometown. I got a hotdog, and after a few bites, I started choking again. The sunflower seed once again blocked my airway. I passed out. My sister Sharri held me upside down as my panicked mom drove us to our little hospital. When we arrived, the doctor hadn't yet arrived to insert a second trach. Lucky for me, a medic who had served in Vietnam was there. He got it done but cut into my vocal cords.

Things became so serious that they sent me to the Mayo Clinic in Rochester, Minnesota. Doctors were researching a new-fangled medical tool, one that had a lighted camera at the end of the scope. My mom brushed aside my dad's objections and signed the consent form. Finally, they discovered the perpetrating seed. After it was removed, I recovered fairly quickly. All told, I spent months in the hospital, sleeping in oxygen tents, pressing a button in my throat to try and talk, and eventually, attending speech therapy. When the ordeal began, my mom didn't even know she was pregnant. By the time it was over, my baby brother, Tim, had been born.

In my hometown, the crazy events of that year made me a celebrity. The story became folklore, and I got a lot of attention.

Saving my life was a career highlight for the small-town family practice doctor. Every Sunday at Mass while I was growing up, Dr. Bennetti would hug me and show me scars on his fingers—I had bitten him so hard during the tracheotomy he had required stitches. Others shared their memories of my ordeal: Someone remembered a doll they gave me while I was in the hospital. People shook their head in disbelief that I survived so long without breathing. I was complimented on my survival as though I was willful or skillful.

I still have a photo of me with that sunflower seed. Living without breath for so long was seen as a most singular achievement. "It's amazing she didn't end up brain-damaged," the doctors would say. And my older brothers would reply, "Oh, but she is." We were that kind of family.

More than fifty years later, when I return to my hometown, people still marvel that the air-deprived girl with damaged vocal cords became a professional speaker.

BREATHING AS METAPHOR

My breath-holding habit started when I was a toddler and never stopped. It was so entrenched that it became a life theme. I was told hundreds of times by coaches in every sport I played: "Don't hold your breath." My diving coach noticed the way I swam furiously to the water's surface after each dive. And then he determined why. I took in a deep gulp of air on the first of a three-step approach to the board and didn't breathe again until I churned to the water's surface with an urgent, slightly panicked gasp.

My chorus teacher was impressed with my ability to hold long notes, and he constantly coached me about the importance of an exhale. When I watched scary movies, I would inhale as I waited for the impending doom of some character, and my friends would have to remind me to let it out. Holding my breath became handy as a survival skill, which I employed during tense moments at home with my family. I didn't want to set anyone off or tip the day from normal to chaos.

There were nights I lay next to my husband, holding my breath so he wouldn't hear me cry or hear the pain that kept me from sleep.

When I held poses on the yoga mat, my teacher would gently touch my back and remind me to breathe. "But I'm trying to hold this warrior," I protested. One day, he pointed out that balanced breathing would strengthen my warrior. Inhaling prepared me for a bold move, while holding my breath weakened my ability to hold it for long periods. By learning to balance the inhale (the internal Warrior) with a great exhale (the internal Healer), I could release the tension and soften into a place that would allow me to go deeper into the pose and maintain it longer. Balanced breathing was counterintuitive—surrender to get stronger. Taking my instructor's advice changed everything about my practice. Exhaling invited in the Healer, dissolving resistance.

That vivid, powerful experience on the yoga mat took on bigger meaning for me. How we improve practice on the mat often shows us better approaches to living off the mat. This breath metaphor, the Warrior and the Healer, helped me notice a lifelong theme of muscling my way through the world. And I could see the need to grow beyond this unsustainable approach to life.

Many of my spiritual teachers talk about the beauty of metaphors in helping people understand themselves and create their own paths to enlightenment. Metaphors have helped me process and integrate experiences at times when reason and logic fall short. Many times, I spin myself crazy trying to understand what happened in my life: What went right? What went wrong? Exactly why did things get so messy? The fact is, we don't really need to fully understand all our experiences; we just need to mine them for useful insights.

For so long, a big, held inhale prepared me for doing hard or scary things, as if the air I took in was infused with courage and fortitude. Holding it was a way to brace myself against a tough challenge or to cope with tense family situations where I feared even the soft sound of an exhale could spark scary emotions. Even today when things get difficult, my first instinct is to inhale and hold—right before I emotionally check out, or get small, or put away my voice.

I saw my strong inhale, the way I could hold it, as useful for unleashing my Warrior. Holding my breath allowed me the illusion of control. But it became clear to me that I also needed to embrace the Healer residing in the exhale.

The Warrior and the Healer, this powerful metaphor, eventually led me to a profoundly rearranged life that included better balance and consistent contentment.

The Warrior

My warrior is fierce.

It's the part of me that challenges conventional wisdom, takes on the toughest issues in the business world, and mounts national stages to talk to big audiences about better answers.

My warrior is ferocious, even when I'm exhausted. It rousts me from much-needed slumber to respond to the crying baby. It shows up for the friends and relatives who are ill or in need. The warrior would never miss a keynote speech, even if it means running on empty and driving through the night. I don't blow deadlines. I succeed in spite of my circumstances.

I excel at being the warrior, at sucking it up and muscling through. I can muster tons of stamina and exhibit great tolerance in difficult, even painful situations. When I am feeling isolated and undersupported, I'm accustomed to making it work anyway.

In tough times, I rarely stop to ask myself if I still want to do hard things or whether I'm enjoying the path I've set out on. I just hold my breath a little longer and overcome.

My warrior also is a source of exhaustion. It overpacks my schedule, fails to set or honor boundaries, and stops prioritizing the useful habits and dedicated practices that build my mental, physical, and spiritual reserves.

I notice this happening first in my breath. My warrior holds her breath.

Every single time when I would retreat to the water, that glorious warrior had suffered defeat. I'd end up at the water in times that love didn't win, exhausted, after I had exceeded my capacity, and it had become too difficult to move in the world while staying true to myself.

I'd often show up at the water profoundly uncentered, off-course, and almost obsessively distracted and drained. My heart was shattered—again. All those amazing feats I perform to keep things going for others, to keep them happy and loving me—what good do they do? I am underappreciated, taken for granted, and unloved.

I planted the battle flag of resentment. I railed at what had become obvious—I can't save the unsavable? I actually have to watch my children hit bottom so they can learn to rise? I can't love enough for both of us? I can't conquer all? Have it all? But I am a warrior!

Make no mistake, I'm not disrespecting the warrior. The warrior is expansive, the birthplace of strength and resilience. A big, held breath creates space for my warrior to thrive. With practice, the inhale opens me up a little more, keeps me going a little longer, diving a little deeper. But natural law decrees that if you don't come up for an exhale, you will explode or implode. And so, I've had to learn the value and beauty of letting my breath go.

The Healer

My time at the water typically starts with a goal of getting stronger and smarter so that I can acquiesce to more. My intention is to become more centered, to armor myself against the profound distractions I have welcomed. I tend to ignore the fact that, at times, I could have just said no to them instead.

As it turned out, more acquiescence wasn't what I needed. It was surrender. For a long time, I didn't understand the difference between the two.

Surrender is not defeat. It isn't giving up. Surrender is giving in and letting the resistance to reality dissolve away. It taps into the nurturing and nourishing elements in the world. It is balanced breath guided by the body's wisdom. In surrender, the long exhale, finally taken, summons the healer. She appears without judgment to gather up the pieces, to integrate them, and to help me make sense of the newest chapter of the journey. Surrender leads to clarity and equanimity.

Getting competent at equanimity is the juice that generates compassion, helps dissolve limits, and initiates a release from past conditioning. I no longer need to be the shivering, breath-holding child who seeks permission to be human.

Equanimity is what I hope to find in meditation, but even then, I notice my warrior asserting herself. When I began meditating, as usual, I wanted to ace it. My goal was laser focus on the mantra, and when I suddenly realized I was instead composing grocery lists, a profane, almost violent unleashing of chastisement would unfold. I lost the mantra! I let an inconvenient and mundane thought disrupt my meditation. Damn it!

With reflection and a little coaching from my teachers, I realized that was missing the point. Sliding away from the mantra is a natural response, and never losing it isn't the goal. Favoring the mantra is the only ask. Practicing love and compassion for oneself in returning to the mantra is experiencing a sort of grace.

The strongest, fiercest, most effective warrior eventually understands the value of release, the soft sigh. A wounded warrior needs time to lay down the armor, to weep, to grieve, to let go.

That's what comes with the exhale—the quiet, the softening, the tears, the sleep: I surrender as a form of strength.

The Healer sees and accepts my limitations. It's shown me how to back away from intensity, to seek wisdom, and to allow perspective to find me. Closure isn't found in the exhale—the inhale is bound to come again. But in that sacred microbeat between exhale and inhale is the space to embrace learning and discover insights. It begins with listening to the inner wisdom that turns us toward those who nurture us and the places that feel safe. Insight and clarity blossom in the light of self-compassion, and balance becomes more effortless. For me, surrender illuminated the path to self-care.

SELF-SOOTHING VS. SELF-CARE

The water is where my healer is most present. At times, my subconscious seems to make it happen even without my conscious participation—and often I am the last to know why I'm really there. It's a process and a path that starts long before I am aware of how much I need self-care. I'm often surprised when I end up there again.

My ongoing attention to balanced breathing helped me to realize that I needed to work on balancing my life. What started as a metaphor to help me hold yoga poses longer and more deeply led me to serious contemplation. I began to realize how much I avoided truly examining the reality of my life and feeling the feelings about that reality. The feelings contained information that clarified reality, and that realization was vital for me to understand that I needed to make different choices.

The healer restored my internal wisdom, illuminating the needs I had choked down, the feelings I kept at bay, and the direction in life I craved but had not followed. The answers were always there, but I needed the Healer and deep self-reflection to see them.

My early attempts at finding the Healer usually came as a way to ease stress: a nap, a great celebration dinner, a glass of wine at the end of the day, claiming time to read a good book, an escape to the spa, the purchase of some luxury item I'd had my eye on. I treated myself as a way to show myself a little kindness. The treats soon escalated to pay-offs. I'd work my ass off, run myself ragged so I could believe I really deserved that long vacation over the holidays, traveling to an exotic location and taking time to lie on the beach, hunkered down with a book for as long as I wanted.

Another favorite self-soothing strategy was to schedule a retreat, thinking it would provide a spiritual pause from the stressful accumulation of my choices. In retreat, I figured I could quickly refill my reserves. But as a wise friend once pointed out—retreat means to break from the enemy. Unfortunately, the enemy was always fully present at my retreats, determined to muscle me through to enlightenment. The enemy was me and my approach to life.

The methods and strategies I used to recover from my life were self-soothing, I came to realize, but not true self-care. The relief that came from self-soothing was fleeting, a temporary respite that couldn't keep life's messiness at bay or make my day-to-day life consistently peaceful.

Self-soothing seemed like a necessity after I went through something tough. I told myself I deserved a reward for surviving, but I began to notice it wasn't building my capacity for happier living. Self-soothing was just a way to numb out or take a short break from all the demands and compromises—the chaotic, unpreferred reality I had co-created.

Those feel-good strategies only delayed the inevitable heartbreak of an exhausted warrior and obscured my inner wisdom. Self-soothing kept me from the deep inner work I needed to do. It kept me from knowing who I was, what I wanted, and from asking important questions of others in my life. I lacked trust in myself to advocate for what I needed in order to live fully.

I enjoy a glass of wine, a day at the spa, a wonderful weekend away to unplug or do some great shopping. But such self-soothing tools are little more than an expedient way to help tolerate the mess. They won't build strong reserves or restore connection to others. And they will likely keep you from a deep knowing of your heart's desire. You won't feel the need to mine your anger for its valuable information. You won't be able to access the intelligence you need to design the life you are meant to be living.

A story—another metaphor—from one of my teachers made me see that maybe my approach could use some spiffing up.

Say you walk down a convenient dark alleyway to get to a required destination—school, or a place of work, perhaps. The alley is unpleasant, unpaved, overflowing with trash, weed-strewn, maybe a few shady characters conducting sketchy business. You're harassed by people demanding spare change.

But a warrior can tolerate the alley! Heck, she can even find a way to appreciate it by focusing on gratitude that she has a home and doesn't have to live there. A warrior can find curiosity or amusement about the players doing their strange business. She can admire the strength she has to successfully navigate the dark passage. A good warrior, carrying a nice glass of wine and dressed in a killer designer outfit, can even find ways to enjoy the stroll through the alley.

But eventually, don't you have to wonder why she doesn't just find a safer, more pleasant, and well-lit way to her destination? Wouldn't that make more sense?

I finally saw the temporary relief of self-soothing would never work in the way I hoped. If I am numbing myself, or temporarily postponing suffering through a retreat from my life, then I've done little but briefly step under a streetlight along my path in the dark alley.

ABANDONING THE ALLEY

Discernment is needed to recognize that it's time for a long, healing exhale—emphasis on healing. I start by noticing when it's become harder for me to be loving and kind. That is my red alert that I have neglected to nurture or nourish myself.

If I don't pick up on the early-warning signals, my irritations grow into anger and resentment. I know it is time to exhale and to ask myself what is exhausting my soul and vanquishing my warrior. Am I keeping the peace with others at the cost of creating a war within myself? What compromises are a form of self-betrayal? Where do I keep saying yes when no would be the healthier answer?

At the water, I allow myself to sit with my anger until it tells me its name.

Most of the time, I find that anger's name is grief, disappointment, or deep sadness. I am called, once again, to recognize that I am not in control. I need to surrender my attempts to fix or change reality and simply feel the grief about a reality that isn't what I hoped for or dreamt of. Grieving moves me toward surrender and acceptance, freeing me from the people-pleasing and the performing for love. I also can see the sadness is about times I dishonored others with my lack of honesty about what I needed or the failure to outline clear boundaries.

With this clarity, I look for the invitation being extended from my frustration, exhaustion, anger. Self-care comes with permission to stop overfunctioning, to stop trying to figure it all out. Where in my life do I need to choose differently?

Compassion is needed to make a graceful and kind return to center. It's a caring that accepts, loves, forgives, and lets go. You don't have to give up on "the ideal." But it is so healing to accept reality, to forgive it and others for what they do and who they are.

The healer has the power to stop the shape-shifting of reality, to clear your vision to what is. The healer helps me ask the right questions: Where am I now? What are my limits? Am I abandoning myself in order to not be abandoned by another? Where have I missed the mark? The healer invites gentle contemplation, a return to what I know but got distracted from. I can recognize myself—and others—as being human.

Recently, distance and solitude have blessed me with a healthier perspective. I want to stop binging on my warrior only to collapse as a puddle into my healer.

What if I could curate a life where retreat from it was no longer required? What if I lived in the mess in a way that built my reserves at the same time? What if I consistently tended to true emotional healing and rid my life of toxic people and activities? Decluttered my life? Created a life with more ease and less friction?

And so, I am curating a life where Warrior and Healer dance with equanimity. The water has become an oasis of nourishing and nurturing. I chose to live at the water rather than living life in a way that yanks me there in temporary, desperate retreat. It's more than symbolic. I moved to the Baja, where I intend to build my dream home in view of the ocean, creating self-care through daily practices.

My wish would be that everyone finds their water—a safe place where they can practice intentional, nourishing self-care. You and I won't walk this path perfectly. We'll lose our balance in the mess of the day. The reset is what matters, and through self-care, the reset happens more quickly, almost simultaneously.

This isn't about another rigorous regimen of self-improvement— that is the last thing my overachieving warrior needs. It is about moving from self-soothing to self-care. And self-care is bigger than a Netflix binge, a nap, or a once-in-a-while massage. Self-care requires, among other things, tapping into the power I've always had: the power of setting boundaries, the power of saying no, the power to forgive, the power to love instead of lash out. My intention is to stop using self-soothing to tolerate the alley and instead let self-care put me on a constantly improving well-lit path. I'm committed to creating gentle disciplines, habits, and devotions that generate a constant supply of energy for me, for the work I love, for the people I love, and for the life I love.

I can let go of mastery so that I can better live in mystery. So can you. Self-care doesn't look the same for everyone, but it comes from the same place. It's about knowing what you need in the moment.

It's understanding that sleep won't help when your soul is

exhausted. It's seeing clearly and acting on your own behalf. It's not expecting others to do what you won't do for yourself. Sit with your anger until it tells you its name. Do the deep emotional work that you need to do to heal yourself. And then set about finding what brings you joy.

Appreciate the inhale *and* the exhale. Welcome the Warrior and the Healer.

Stop holding your breath.

THE EVOLUTION FROM SELF-SOOTHING TO SELF-CARE

Creating a life that you don't need to retreat from means more focus on self-care instead of constant attempts at self-soothing, which are a form of pampering or numbing out at the expense of feeling and honoring your emotions. Self-care isn't the same for everyone. It's about what you need in this moment, and the next moment, and the moment after that. Self-care is composed of the actions you take to ensure that you have a consistent supply of energy for the people you love, the work you love, and the life you love. Consider this menu of self-care strategies and see what might be worth integrating.

Self-Care Is:

- Getting plentiful sleep, eating well, and moving your body.

- Curating, organizing, and decluttering your life to be more effortless and to remove friction.

- Listening to your inner voice and paying attention to your body and the information it provides—getting to know your own "full body yes and full body no."

- Remembering who you are. What do you like? What do you most enjoy doing in your spare time—just for you? What brings you joy? If you're unsure, look to your childhood for clues.

- Speaking your truth instead of telling others what they want to hear.

- Understanding there are times you come first, which means being willing to sometimes have people feel disappointed in you.

- Knowing your social needs and limits and setting boundaries.

- Keeping in your life only those people who are energy-building.

- Maintaining the actions, habits, and dedications you perform to take care of your physical, emotional, spiritual, and mental needs with equanimity.

- Continuing to learn and to have an impact in your work life. Having a job that makes you happy and establishing boundaries at work, staying relevant and keeping up with the times.

- Appreciating your ability to get through hard things AND giving yourself permission to choose another way.

- Giving yourself a break and refusing to feel guilty about it.

- Letting go of a toxic relationship that you know is no longer right for you.

- Facing and fixing your toxic behaviors.

- Curating a life you love instead of settling for constant stress and unhappiness.

- Therapy can be a great act of self-care.

FEEL ALL YOUR FEELS

L OL.
    WTF?!?

Broken-heart emoji.

How many times have you seen something hilarious on social media and immediately forwarded it to your friends with an "LOL"? So many times, right? But answer honestly: Did you *really* laugh out loud? Did you feel the humor so deeply that a good guffaw erupted from the depths of your gut before you passed the meme along? And seriously, have you ever ROTFL—rolled on the floor laughing—because you just couldn't stop?

Do you really *feel* your feelings? Or are they more of an intellectual experience? "Oh, that is funny, lol. I should share it with my friends."

How many times have people come to you in an emotional state (or vice versa) and the conversation immediately becomes a brainstorm designed to put that feeling out, as if it is a fire that might consume the forest? You feel angry, but instead of sitting with the anger wholeheartedly and listening from your heart to receive the wisdom it could reveal, you mentally catalogue the reasons you have every right to feel angry, or conversely, set about talking yourself out of it?

If you're like most people, instead of feeling your feels you're allowing the ego to bypass your emotional experience by intellectualizing it. The world offers myriad ways of doing this, especially now that we spend more time on social media and in electronic meetings and less time connecting deeply with others face-to-face.

Getting fluent in feelings—actually embodying them with a big lusty laugh or a good cry, for example—is a key competency for successful adulthood and for thriving in spite of the mess.

Emotions are vital. They are signals telling us to pay attention to something important. Those situations that make you feel deeply uncomfortable? Those times you're anxious, angry, yearning, confused, in pain? Those feelings aren't clues that you have a problem; they're indicators that you have a life. Often, we even rush past those "feel good" emotions like contentment, joy, exhilaration, and reverence without allowing ourselves to steep in them awhile.

Emotions are about being alive—about showing up and interacting fully with the world. Sometimes they are visceral and instinctive. And in many other instances, they spring from your illusions of being separate or alone. Sometimes feelings are a sign you're unable to view the world clearly. You're blocked from seeing love, the only real truth.

You'll never change the fact that life can be hard. You have to get over the notion that being human should be easy. Being human is hard, not because you are doing it wrong; it's a challenge because you're doing it right.

To live happily in the mess, it's essential to learn to breathe your feelings in, be with them fully, and let them pass on through. Feelings don't have to rule your life or become an emotional bog you can never climb out of. The more adept you become at being fully present for your emotions, the more quickly you'll find the relief of release. Feelings are like the weather, constantly changing and, with a little time and acknowledgment, blowing through.

Although I highly recommend feeling all the feels and absorbing their innate intelligence, you don't necessarily always have to trust them completely. Noticing your feelings when they're moderate is a wonderful time to examine them for the information they're delivering. An emotional response to circumstances can be an invitation to help you understand when you should draw closer and when it might be better to keep your distance.

When feelings are intense—or out of proportion to the circumstance—the message they're delivering is even more important. Feel those strong emotions, sit with them, let them talk to you. Sometimes the intensity is a sign that multiple feelings and moments are present at the same time. It mostly happens when you experience the "now" in combination with past wounds, for example, the experience of the child who felt helpless and afraid. Feelings also can be amped up when they're layered with fear or anxiety about the future, which can never be known.

Feelings that are inclined to linger could be information about things you have too long ignored. They could be an indication of recurring themes in your life that are helping create unpreferred circumstances. Are you clinging to the familiar because you fear how a change might affect your future? Sometimes sticking with the familiar patterns of the past is a way to keep fears associated with the present or future at bay.

LEARNING TO FEEL THOSE FEELS

Here is a beginner's guide to feeling your emotions thoroughly, with a whole heart. Learning to feel—and listen to—your feels will contribute mightily to your ability to live happily and authentically in the mess.

1. Notice the feeling arising.

2. Notice when you begin thinking about what you're feeling, as the ego takes over with its narration of stories, limiting beliefs, and tried-and-true predictions of what's next.

3. Notice and stop! You are thinking your feelings.

4. Focus on your breath, which disconnects you from the thinking mind and directs your presence to your body's sensations.

5. Name the feeling. Ask the sensation, the feeling, the emotion to tell you its name. Not the story, just the name.

6. Stay with the sensation. Allow the feeling to embody you— cry, laugh, shake, scream, moan, smile, make a face that corresponds to the emotion. Give the feeling physical help to facilitate its dissipation.

7. Notice how your mind wants to return to story—assigning blame, painting you as the victim, naming others as villains. Return to breath, physical awareness, and the embodiment of the feeling.

8. Get curious when you're reactive. Do you have a wound to heal?

9. Continue deep breathing, and use compassionate self-talk, as if you were comforting a child. In many ways, you are.

10. Practice staying present longer each time—lean into the feeling. Let it exist and trust that it will eventually pass through.

11. Observe the changes as the feeling shifts and moves, perhaps from anger, to disappointment, to sadness.

12. Notice, as the feeling passes, that you have survived.

GENEROSITY

I got my sister a new liver. And then I waited for the full-blast warm shower of gratitude.

My family has been through a lot of hard times, but this ordeal had been among the most challenging. After years of showing up, helping, intervening, and insisting, my siblings and I pulled off what felt like the miracle of the century. We got my older sister Sharri a liver transplant. We did it because we love her. We all were loath to lose another family member prematurely. We wanted to save and extend her life. She had been ill and struggling for a long time, and we wanted her back.

I was beyond excited when we finally managed to pull it off. We'd busted through so many obstacles, including the medical bureaucracy and her reluctance to follow the medical protocols required to be on the transplant list. The experience was emotional and exhausting, and I was elated when she came through the surgery with good results. We entered round two of helping her recover and getting the care she needed.

But soon I noticed a little speck of fly in the ointment of post-surgery exhilaration, a fly that kept thrashing and squealing. A tiny part of my grand plan had failed to materialize.

The expected blast of gratitude never came.

EARNING LOVE

We were a big family—seven kids—with two loving, supportive, and busy parents. Between my family and my small town village, we were all well taken care of. And, like any family, the dynamics of our household included varying strains of dysfunction. You know that saying that shit flows downhill? Well, I was the second-youngest kid. You can figure it out.

If you grew up like I did, help was a commodity rarely offered for free. Any favor asked became a transaction. I learned early on to keep my needs to myself, to avoid bothering already overwhelmed people. My experience was that some kind of payment would be extracted for any help proffered.

Our family system was built on implied threats, pointed glares, tense body language, raised voices, simmering silences, narrowed eyes, and occasional explosive rants. For me, this often created confusion and anger as I tried to pick my way through the minefield, hoping not to be blown up. I learned to be left alone by not asking for much. My strategy for earning love and gold stars was to be good.

My skills in people-pleasing were sharp, ready to be wielded in an instant. I never caused trouble with my parents. At school, I was the overachiever who finished work early. At the teacher's request, I took a classmate who struggled with schoolwork under my wing. I was so helpful at home and abroad that I sometimes ached from the effort. My good-girl, people-pleasing behavior earned me approval, which satisfied my underlying need for attention and love. It also left me with a nagging, uncomfortable question: Did people love me for who I am? Or was love transactional, based on what I did for others and on how little I needed from them?

My relationship with my sister Sharri, who was near the top of the family food chain, had always been extra complicated. Her frequent assignment as a teenager was to care for her baby sister. Maybe she loved *me*, but she definitely didn't love being saddled with the role of pseudo-mom, and she figured it gave her license to be mean to me. As a kid, I lived in fear of pissing her off, losing her love. Even after I became a competent, successful adult, the baby sister maintained a little room in my heart, always longing to prove she was worthy of love, respect, and admiration.

When Sharri encountered troubling times, I consistently showed up for her when she demanded it, and eventually, even when she didn't ask. When her husband was seriously ill, I often flew a multiple-city circuit to get them settled in for his treatments. After he died, I took monthly four-hour flights and spent long weekends helping her settle the estate, pay bills, and put her finances in order—for years. When she was in a bind, when her friends called because her health was declining and she wouldn't take care of herself, when she had to be hospitalized, I booked the flights and arrived on her doorstep to make order out of chaos. My dying mother had told me, "Be sure to take care of your sister." For years, I had done that work in addition to my responsibilities of raising eight sons and running a demanding business.

Now my siblings and I had literally saved her from sure death after her illness had severely damaged her liver, had caused bouts of internal bleeding, and had made her partially blind. The successful transplant banished immediate death from her doorstep. Thus, I waited for my reward, for her to admit what an awesome sister I had always been, to beg for my forgiveness for all the times she'd been mean to me, and for her to acknowledge, at last, that I was a freaking saint.

Not only was the acknowledgment withheld, my siblings and I were treated to a kind of behavior that we hadn't before experienced. I had hoped she'd see our efforts as giving her a second chance. I'd imagined she would want to help the world, to make amends, to tell her story so more people would donate organs. Instead, she wouldn't even meet us halfway in completing her recovery. She bucked doctors' orders at every turn. She assigned negative and unfair motives to actions designed to help her. She accused us of abandoning her while she was in the hospital, even though one of us was with her every night during her five-month stay. When the rehabilitation facility ejected her for refusing to participate in her treatment, she came to live at my house. She said hateful things to us and to the caregivers, who often refused to return. She left us with huge bills for her care and then accused us of stealing from her. As we worked to make sure she was taken care of, my siblings and I were often emotionally exhausted and in tears brought on by her words and actions.

Yes, we saved my sister's life, and of course I have no regrets about that. I would do it again, and I'm happy she's alive. But I was shocked at how furious I felt when she engaged in what I saw as grossly inappropriate behavior in the wake of the big save. HOW DARE SHE?

Reality once again had thrown me for a loop. After all I had done, all the ways I had shown up, all the strings I had pulled, all the care we had invested—she was going to deprive me of my well-earned redemption and glory? After investing financial resources, emotional energy, and time into getting my sister help she clearly needed, she had the nerve to deny us our happy-ever-after moment? To see me as a villain?

As I wrestled with the injustice and pain of her reaction, it slowly dawned on me that the help we had insisted on providing had never been requested. While Sharri felt free to ask for my help in managing the day-to-day details of her life, my prescription was that she needed to drastically change her lifestyle so she could manage her own life. She hadn't asked for that help, and in hindsight, she didn't seem ready for it.

Maybe acquiescing to her demands in the name of helping wasn't really about help at all. Nor was my insistence on delivering help she hadn't requested.

I had believed my actions sprang from pure, loving generosity. But on reflection, I realized her reaction to my unasked-for help was something I'd seen before. I'd been hurt by others in the same way. Sometimes I became so determined to be generous that I worked harder at others' success than they did. Then, after all I'd done, I'd be shocked when they treated me poorly. I thought about all the times I felt unappreciated. Why did so many people I care about take me for granted? How did I end up disappointed, resentful, and burned out instead of energized and grateful?

As I sat with my anger, the focus shifted from what I felt Sharri had done to me to an examination of my own contribution to this lifelong pattern. Uncomfortable questions started bubbling up. As the questions changed, everything changed.

Why did I keep showing up for Sharri? Why was I *allowing her* to treat me poorly? Why was I working harder for her recovery than she was? Why was I so insistent on proffering help that didn't seem wanted and was rarely appreciated?

In the wake of "Why are they treating me like shit?" better questions rose up: Why do I stay? Why do I drive myself crazy trying to figure out how to help other people get better or be better? Why am I always spinning, constantly seeking ways to be cooler and smarter and more giving so people would approve of me? The shift in the questions provided the breakthrough. Maybe my help, in the words of writer Anne Lamott, was just "the sunny side of control."

BOUNDARIES: SUNNY SIDE OF SELF-CONTROL

I do love being generous. I treasure that quality in myself. Helping others, contributing with no strings attached, gives me great satisfaction and reward. Generosity is a big part of who I am.

I have been given so much. I believe in abundance, and when I can use my resources to help someone else, it's abundance reborn. Your joy is my joy.

And yet, I can't deny the presence of an underlying fear that if I don't keep giving, people won't keep choosing me. I had to confront something about myself that was difficult: If I am affronted when I'm not paid off with praise and appropriate gratitude, aren't I just being manipulative? Doesn't that sully the gift?

Without established boundaries, generosity isn't really about giving—it's an ego-riddled way to prove I am lovable and worthy. My experience with my sister was the most egregious example, but it wasn't the only one. When I gave without boundaries, my generosity typically led to self-betrayal. My eyes began opening to the ways I often overgave, abandoning myself so another wouldn't abandon me.

My motives for helping my older sister definitely were not malignant, but maybe they hadn't been as pure as I would have wished. I kept showing up partly to heal old wounds and earn approval. The cost of that kind of giving can be deep loneliness because others don't see who I really am. Without honesty about the underlying intentions of my generosity, my authentic self couldn't be revealed. How could I be seen and loved for who I am if I wasn't willing to let go of the transaction and the ways I performed for love?

Sometimes unrequested help isn't helpful. Neither is continuing to show up when help is unwelcomed or consistently refused. True generosity is that which I do joyfully and peacefully, without resentment and without expectation of a payoff. It creates its own surplus.

For example, one day after work I was ready to head home for my daily walk around the lake. I noticed a frustrated colleague who was struggling with an assignment. Although I knew it would mean sacrificing my walk, I offered to help him figure out an approach to a tough training assignment with a difficult client. I grabbed us a beverage, coached him, gave him my presence, energy, and advice. I let him know I believed in him. In the aftermath, I kept quiet about our time together. This authentic generosity left us both feeling full, satisfied, and energized.

Another day, a major deadline was looming in less than twenty-four hours. A different colleague seemed moody and worried. Though I had no time to spare, I put aside my work and invited her to take a break. As we sipped beverages, I coached, advised, and offered strategies, even though I was stressed about my own deadline. I wanted to appear generous and supportive to impress others. I wanted her to like me—or at least not dislike me. Plus, I figured she'd owe me in the future. The next morning, someone asked about my project. I made sure everyone knew I'd met my deadline by staying up late and sacrificing sleep because of my "gift" of supporting a colleague. And for extra measure, I let it slip that she didn't even thank me for helping her land a $20,000 contract.

The dark side of that generosity left me feeling resentful, tired, and depleted.

THE ROOTS OF OVERGIVING

My sister's behavior, in my view, violated basic boundaries of human decency, and I wasn't the only one who saw it that way. She rarely expressed gratitude, and she had long refused to see how she was contributing to her own problems. That begged the question: In the face of that, why had I kept showing up?

It wasn't hard to figure out that my childhood wounds hadn't fully healed. In our family, relationships tended to be transactional—an ask was the start of a negotiation. With six siblings, for example, it was a rare treat to have control of the television set. On occasion, I would be enjoying the antics of the castaway crew of *Gilligan's Island* when one of my older brothers would come in and change the channel. "Hey!" I would protest. "I'm watching that!" His response: "Give me two bucks, and I'll let you keep watching it."

From a very young age, I was a really hard worker, and earning my own money was a big deal. My brother paid me a dollar for helping him with his paper route. One of my siblings would demand that I turn it over. I would refuse. Negotiations ensued. Okay, then fork over fifty cents. No. Buy me a candy bar. No. Sometimes they would block the door to our only bathroom until I coughed up a toll. I had zero power in my family hierarchy.

When I complained to my mom, she suggested I take the high road. "Turn the other cheek," she would say. "Don't let them get to you. You have maturity and abilities that they don't have. Be better than they are."

Even if I tried to set a boundary, it didn't seem worth it. Needs and wants looked like a bother for already overwhelmed people. I knew I'd end up paying in some way. In the end, it was all about the exchange—keep quiet and tolerate the demands and badgering so that you don't add to the family chaos. Give up something—money, time, dignity—to keep the peace. To be loved. To be chosen.

I compensated by overgiving, which also stunted my ability to accept help. I felt the need to always be one up and never in debt. By offering help and refusing to accept it from others, I felt in control. It was better to be owed. As Anaïs Nin said, "I was always ashamed to take. So I gave. It was not a virtue. It was a disguise."

As a kid, I didn't have much choice about leaving the family. I had to stay because I couldn't survive on my own. But as an adult, my experience with Sharri underscored a big "aha!" I didn't have to stay, and when I continued to show up in the face of her behavior, it wasn't loving, and it wasn't her fault. That was on me. I had to face the truth that I was paying a high internal price to buy the love of others, to ensure they wouldn't leave me.

For too long, I'd let some people walk all over me while they complained about how flat I was. I could see that setting appropriate boundaries is one way to establish self-worth. I wanted to purify my generosity and offer gifts with great expectancy but without expectations.

Blaming others for my emotional experience was a trap I didn't want to get caught in. Awareness of my wounds, and the coping strategies I used to avoid or heal them, was essential. Developing awareness added knowledge and layers to my experience and helped me to better understand how the strategies came about:

- Being the "good girl" kept me out of harm's way.

- Staying quiet or compliant meant I didn't add to the overwhelm of my mom and family.

- When I asked for help or justice, I got bad advice that just helped others avoid conflict: Turn the other cheek— don't let them see they got to you. To whom much is given, much is expected.

- I must perform for love.

These things are real, but self-victimization is a big distraction from setting boundaries that help me manage my energy. Just because I grew up with an overgiving mindset doesn't mean I couldn't change these patterns for the last half of my life. For too long, I've been fooling myself and others because I've believed false storylines. They took a while to bubble up from subconscious to consciousness so I could reject them:

"I am not enough."

"I am loved for what I do, not who I am."

"To keep people choosing me, I have to keep them clear on the value I bring."

In too many cases, giving enabled me to have the illusion of control of how others saw me. Sometimes my generosity was a way to prove I was kind, smart, successful, superior. I gave in order to prove others wrong about who they thought I was, and I refused to receive because it required vulnerability. In some cases, I have fooled people into thinking I am an incredibly giving person, when too often it was my unconscious way of covering up fear and insecurities. Not asking and not receiving was my go-to defense mechanism to avoid pain.

I can recognize that true help is freely given, not a ransom demand. "Help is the sunny side of control" encapsulates what I've been wrestling with for years. It has taken too long, but I feel like I'm ready to accept this bold truth: *When help is mostly about me and what I want the other person to do in return, it is not help. It's manipulation, expectation, or an attempt to con-*

trol. And control makes me feel safe even though it endangers my soul.

After significant inner work, I intend to grow up. Setting and enforcing boundaries requires me to know that I am truly lovable and kind and worthy. It is up to me to teach others what I will and will not allow—what I am willing and not willing to give.

It's clear to me now that not all giving is created equal. On the surface, gifts may appear the same, but their roots will generate completely different energy. Generosity born from insecurity becomes a way to earn validation. Gifts that emanate from scarcity can become a mental accounting system of what you are owed, which breeds entitlement. Acts of giving from this place lead to depletion.

Understanding the roots of giving has enabled me to be more aware of when I'm giving from a place of woundedness, fear, and guilt. Checking in with myself before I give has been helpful. If my "gift" is rooted in those emotions, I reassess. I need to change my intention or rethink the gift.

When I feel resentment or anger bubbling up after an act of generosity, that's my red flag. I know I need to be clear about my intentions, examine my boundaries, and possibly reinforce them. Boundaries outline the sweet spot where I can love and take care of me and others at the same time.

True generosity springs from love, not from getting credit. You are not trying to earn anything or receive a return on investment. You're not keeping a tab. It feels inspiring, vibrant, and satisfying.

I am committed to healing a wound that was the basis of much of my energy-sapping behavior—from overachieving in life and work to overgiving in relationships to prove my worthiness and lovability. I am learning to lean in to the vulnerability of asking for what I need and to practicing receiving. Accepting others' help is another form of generosity.

No success, no achievement, no compliment or accolade will heal old wounds or bestow a sense of being worthy. Knowing that you are enough is an inner game. It comes from accepting yourself fully, from being your own source of love and abundance. I have to know that I am worthy of love and validation for who I am. Period.

Now my practice centers on stopping the hypervigilance about what others need and on offering help with no strings attached. Establishing boundaries is a new and radical behavior, and it's also so hard. I have to push myself to receive help, support, and care from others without feeling that I must repay a debt that was never demanded.

I can love people, be present to them, and remember they have the resources to figure it out. My intention is to telegraph confidence in them and their ability to find their own solutions. I'm willing to help problem-solve, but I don't need to provide an instant fix. If you're working harder for others' happiness and success than they are, stop. That's a recipe for misery and resentment. Capable people can ask for help if they need it.

Setting boundaries became simpler when I decided what kind of life I wanted and began saying no to the things that didn't support that life. I created a prayer for myself that I repeat almost every day:

"Please release me from the need for love, approval, and appreciation. If I don't need those things, I can give freely from my heart."

ARE YOU OVERGIVING?

Are you providing help that wasn't requested, not charging what you are worth, or consistently being the "fixer" in your relationships? Generosity is a wonderful quality when it comes from the right intention. Volunteering has even been shown to improve your mental health. However, without clear intentions, giving can be exhausting over time and will not build a foundation for healthy relationships.

If you have become used to overgiving your energy and time, it can be hard to see your part in the pattern. To keep your giving coming from a healthy, generous place, the following exercise could help you determine the assumptions and motivations of giving.

1. **What Is the State of Your Giving?**

    For a week, focus on the times you give your time, energy, and money to others. Write down each instance, along with how you felt when you agreed to give and how you felt afterward. At the end of the week, review the instances and ask yourself:

    - What giving felt satisfying, and what giving left you feeling depleted?

    - In which environments did you tend to give? Home? Work? Community?

    - What moods led to overgiving?

- What could you have done instead of the activity you did for someone else?

2. **What Was Your Underlying Need?**

Reflecting on your list can provide insight into motive. Giving too much in a relationship can be an act of manipulation. For example: "I proofread my colleague's report because I want her to like me" or "I gave a loved one money to avoid the silent treatment that comes if I say no."

Identifying reasons why you say "yes" when you want to say "no" might help you find other ways to meet a need or to let go of the need altogether. Communicate in healthier ways by summoning the courage to explain that you're setting boundaries and why.

3. **What Core Belief Gets in the Way of Saying No?**

Limiting core beliefs are assumptions that you have mistaken as truth and can keep you engaged in unhealthy behavior. Excavate and examine your assumptions. For example, a core belief could be "If I don't give them what they ask for, I won't be liked." Or "If I don't help them, they won't be able to do it on their own."

4. **Use the Timeout Rule.**

When you are tempted to give to others to avoid duress, consider a response like, "Let me think about it and get back to you." Give yourself the gift of time so you can consider how you feel about the request. Doing so before you extend generosity will help you be more honest in your helping.

5. **Balance Your Perspective.**

If you want to say no but are struggling, alleviate the fear with an exercise:

- Write down the worst thing that could happen if you say no to the person or experience.

- Write down the exact opposite.

- End with finding a thought that is exactly in the middle—this thought will help you find perspective.

- Notice how much better you feel about the possibility of saying no.

   For example, *"I can't say no because my boss will think I am lazy and fire me." "If I say yes, my boss will think I am assertive and promote me." Balanced thought in the middle? "I might annoy my boss because he'll have to find someone else, but I won't lose my job over this."*

6. **Get Comfortable with Being Uncomfortable.**

This takes practice. Doing something out of character can feel scary in the beginning. If you feel discomfort, anxiety, or fear saying "yes" to only those things that you wholeheartedly want to do or give, it's a good sign that you are taking risks and growing. Acknowledge and feel the feelings you are having.

7. **Get Support.**

Share your intentions with a few trusted others who are good at setting healthy boundaries. Ask them for feedback when you think you may be overgiving. Rely on them to bring perspective to the situations and to suggest scripts you can use until you become skilled in setting boundaries.

EMERGE EVOLVED,
NOT TRAUMATIZED

In my first undergraduate program, I studied international relations and became fascinated with an emerging economic concept called microlending. The idea was that lending small amounts of money or other resources to the right people at the right time could alter their lives for the positive. For instance, giving a few cows to a family in a small village could supply milk in the short term, and as they raised more cattle, they could pay it forward with the gift of a cow or two to others nearby. Small, simple acts could change the economic destiny of people who were struggling.

With all the eagerness of youth, I became zealous about doing good in the world. A friend and I traveled to Africa with a group of like-minded college students who were interested in using creative economic development tools to help people. When we arrived, I was struck by the meagerness of our accommodations. Although I knew we had some of the best rooms available, they were cramped and sparsely furnished—small beds and a tiny sink and toilet.

When my roomie saw my reaction—"Hey, Dorothy, we're not in Kansas anymore!"—she proudly began to unpack. I'd traveled with a duffle bag. She had hauled over a considerable amount of luggage. I had assumed her more expansive suitcases contained gifts for our hosts and others we'd be working to help. While she had brought some of those things, she also brought along a bunch of stuff to ease any deprivations we might encounter. She pulled out twenty-four packets of hot chocolate, enough to last the entire trip, and invited me to find water to heat up so I could enjoy a cup. As I laid out my down sleeping bag on the little bed, she smugly pulled out an extra pillow for my comfort. As our trip went on, she seemed to have packed almost everything I and others in our group might possibly need—aspirin, Band-Aids, heartburn medicine, extra socks, sewing kits. We began calling her Mary Poppins, because her bags were seemingly bottomless and magical.

After a while, I found this a bit irritating, and then borderline offensive. Her days seemed to be more focused on replicating the life we lived at home than soaking up the experience. My goal was to immerse myself in our work and identify the ways we could change lives!

As I sat for days, listening to adolescent girls and young women talk about their lives, my ethnocentric views delivered a sharp jab to my chin. The resulting whiplash revealed my innocence, ignorance, and arrogance as I realized I didn't have answers and the best solutions—the women I was talking to did.

Our goal had been to help the young women in the community

become more economically prosperous. As we conversed, I discovered our ideas of helping had the potential to either brand them as unsuitable for marriage because of wealth disparity or, alternately, make them more valuable "property" for men. What they really wanted, I learned, was sanitary products so they could continue attending school during their menstrual periods. They needed additional school uniforms so they didn't need to split days with their sisters who also were attending school. Access to birth control or good health care were far more valuable to them than a cow, which could be stolen, die, or become prey for other animals. The "gift" of a cow would mean one more mouth to feed until a herd got established—if it did—and that would take years.

That trip undid me. My naivete was that I could swoop in and positively change the lives of others, but in the end, I was the one who changed for the better. The experience taught me how little I knew and set me on a path of unlearning what I thought I did know.

A few weeks after we returned, my friend and I received forms in the mail asking for feedback about the trip. We decided to save ourselves another trip to the mailboxes by filling the forms out together at the mail center. I wrote ecstatically about my experience, raving about our lodging, the food, and providing detailed examples of what I'd learned and the personal growth the trip had spurred. As I wrote, my friend grew impatient. "My form is filled out," she said. "What is taking you so long?" She glanced at my answers, which sparked an interesting conversation. Though we had been in the same place at the same time, we clearly had been on very different trips. She felt the experience didn't live up to the expectations outlined in the informational brochure. She rated the experience as subpar. She had a list of things upon which the organizers could improve.

We had started the trip with common characteristics: big hearts and a strong desire to help others. She brought everything she *knew* with her, along with familiar accoutrements that would spare her discomfort. She worked so hard to avoid being traumatized by the trip that she didn't allow herself to open up to the largesse all around her.

I had stumbled into the trip also believing I knew something. When it turned out I didn't know much, I allowed myself to become undone. Whether this happened because I was born prewired for curiosity or because some previously hidden inner wisdom emerged, I can't say. But I'm grateful for the trip's powerful and rewarding life lesson: The act of unlearning can be as important and necessary as the act of learning.

In my experience, unlearning is a vital competency to a rich and relevant life. Unlearning is not passive. It requires a willingness to hold on to several seemingly contradictory ideas at once. You live with cognitive dissonance until you find the space to let go of what you thought you knew in order to edge closer to something bigger and truer.

During 2020, I thought a lot about my college experience as the world roiled from a pandemic and the U.S. was convulsed with social uprisings. As crises and challenges erupted in what felt like endless waves, I wondered how I could have been so unaware of my own privilege. Why hadn't I more actively delved into my hidden biases? It was a time of great unlearning. I found myself sitting with the discomfort of not knowing, not mastering, not leading, and honestly, not even knowing what the next right step to take would be.

I observed so many people who seemed traumatized by the uncertainty and changes. From my perspective, underdeveloped resiliency was a side effect of being shielded in the past from challenges and this very illusion of certainty. The mystery of what was unfolding seemed to prompt a closing down instead of an opening up. This was exemplified in a coaching conversation I had with a physician in the early days of the COVID-19 crisis. He reached out, utterly exhausted, after having worked his tenth straight shift in an emergency room in New York City.

"Cy, this is crazy," he said. "We don't even know what this is. I am not able to help the patients coming in. I have lost my ability to add value. I used to know what to do. I could almost predict what would be coming our way in a typical shift. I knew how I would get to work, where I would park, where I could pick up my favorite breakfast after I finish my shift.

"Now I don't know anything. I have lost my confidence. I don't know if my team and I can do this. We aren't that brilliant. We're not that good in the face of this health crisis."

He sounded thoroughly defeated. He was trying to muscle through the challenge with heroics and routine and had lost connection to his authentic resilience.

I recalled research I had done previously while studying accountability, which had revealed true resilience isn't about stamina or heroics. Resiliency is highest in those who have the biggest network of positive relationships. People who found resilience relied on an established, healthy network from which to crowdsource strategies and techniques. Resiliency was also marked by those willing to be vulnerable and ask for help. This doctor was doing that with me. I needed to suggest a strategy change to return his confidence.

The doctor had expertise and mastery, and he knew a lot about medical care. But his confidence was anchored in predictability and certainty, which had proven to be an illusion. COVID-19 made that clear. What if he would re-anchor his confidence not based solely on his own abilities but in the genius of the collective? He didn't and couldn't personally know what was best in such unprecedented times, but he could figure it out with others. Could he answer the invitation made by his current reality to anchor his confidence in something bigger and absolutely accessible to him in the present?

That's what he did. He stood up at forums centered on COVID in his medical center and began conversations that led to the sharing of discoveries among nurses and staff in the ICU, which informed treatments in the emergency room. He tapped into a network of peers outside his medical center to share and receive real-time learnings about new, more effective treatments. Rather than feeling defeated, he began to feel energized. He was committed to learning as fast as the virus was mutating. He was part of something bigger—connected to a network that included experts in the World Health Organization, the Centers for Disease Control, and the National Institutes of Health. The energy he was pouring into figuring out what to do on his own was reinvested into connecting and collaborating with others. Instead of venting about doomsday, he became a contributor to solutions, imagining with others possible positive outcomes. By sharing his knowledge and experience with others, the doctor boosted his skills, his confidence, and his energy. As Albert Einstein said, together we are genius—a secret the most resilient are well aware of.

What the pandemic revealed to him in his hour of "falling apart" was humbling. His impending case of burnout was caused not just by a patient overload but because he was clinging to older, comfortable approaches in a world that had radically changed. His pain caused him to reach out for help, and he did the self-reflection and work that led to his evolution. It allowed him to fully function in a tough time and a changed environment. Instead of emerging from the crisis impaired, he came through it much improved.

When faced with extreme disruption, contemplation and introspection can be life-changing. "What is my current reality revealing to me?" The COVID-19 lockdown—an external confinement—gave me the opportunity to look inward to discover the prisons I had created in my own mind, my inner world, my closest relationships, and I began to ask others to do the same, including my team, those I coached, and the people in my audiences. As I have cracked to my staff, "Why let a good pandemic go to waste?"

What does crisis reveal about your relationship with solitude or uncertainty? What did the pandemic show you about the state of your boundaries or willingness to ask for help? When you were unable to do all the things you did before, what did you discover that your previous "busyness" hid?

My intention isn't to minimize the hurt, suffering, and loss of so many people. But what often gets forgotten in extreme times is the invitation that life offers in the same moment. If you're willing to look for it, you will be shown the place you need to grow in order to be ready for what comes next. Doing the work of observing what is revealed about you and growing beyond it ensures you are ready to play full out in the next set of challenges life offers.

So many people lived with the assumption that our families, our children, our colleagues would be traumatized by these events. They saw the only options and outcomes to unprecedented circumstances as stress and trauma, as if what was happening had a predetermined, unchangeable destiny. Those who accepted that premise tended to respond accordingly. Some pined for the past and fought to reinforce what they knew. Some were overwhelmed by despair and pessimism. Some, desperate for normal life, risked their and others' health and violated their ethics to get what they thought they needed or deserved.

Others turned to self-care, contemplation, and finding different ways to connect with others. They reached out for help and to help. People were innovative and willing to live radically simplified lives within the external constraints of the times. I saw people do something revolutionary—they intentionally curated the lives they wanted to carry with them into whatever comes next. These are the people who will emerge from their unpreferred circumstances evolved instead of traumatized.

There is a plethora of research from the field of positive psychology that suggests people, depending on their responses, can emerge from a traumatic event, or traumatic times, with posttraumatic growth. This is different from Post-Traumatic Stress Disorder, or PTSD. That is real—it can be diagnosed, is painful to live with, and no one chooses it.

However, it's not a predetermined outcome of trauma. Research suggests it's not even the most likely option. The choices we make and the actions we take have a lot to do with whether we come through tough times transformed through personal growth or stay stuck, reinforcing our negative views of a frightening, uncontrollable world.

The differentiating factor is the intentional mining of your experience to notice what is being revealed and taking steps that will aid your own evolution. Another key factor is hope. While tending to the very real grief of the moment, the boldest act is to imagine multiple positive possibilities. Questioning the assumed doomsday outcome loosens the ego's grip on your view of the world. Suggesting a better future doesn't negate the very real pain of today. Both things can be true. Today we hurt, *and* we can choose to do things that could change the future in a positive way.

In an unpreferred reality, people tend to think that the solution is to change the current reality. Many times, that isn't possible or within our control, which initiates an enormous investment of time and energy railing against reality, complaining and wishing it were different. As I always say, you can argue with reality, but you will lose that argument only 100 percent of the time.

Complaining about the present and wishing for a preferred future isn't an effective strategy. It will keep you stuck and lead to burnout. But there is a small space between those poles where you can take action and heighten the opportunity for impact. Self-reflective questions help: What is the invitation being made to me in this moment? What can I do in this moment that would help? How can I elevate my view? What is my opportunity to grow and prepare for a better future? How could I step into the power I already have to imagine a different future and make choices to connect the current to the future?

Tough times are still our times. When epic circumstances erupt, powerful choices can be made that will spur Post-Traumatic Growth.

A BAD DAY FOR THE EGO IS A GOOD DAY FOR THE SOUL

The pandemic and the social unrest were challenging, and they also were full of invitations to evolve. I got another dose of harsh reality in the aftermath of the murder of George Floyd in Minneapolis, captured on video and commanding the attention of a horrified nation. His death initiated a flood of events that put an even brighter spotlight on the state of racism in our nation. As we sheltered at home, we were earning a graduate degree in police brutality, social and economic inequities, structural and systemic racism, and white privilege. I was confronted with more honest versions of the country's history in which I felt complicit. That young college student still inside me came alive. I felt the need to help.

One day I opened up my Instagram to a request. Some well-meaning people had organized a plan for "IG influencers" to go silent so that the voices of people of color could be amplified. If we silenced our considerable platforms, IG's algorithms might put the messages of POC in front of more eyeballs.

I was not only glad to help, I was proud of myself for agreeing to silence myself to raise the volume of others. I wanted to be a good ally in as many ways as possible.

Then the comments of those with deep experience, folks who'd been doing the heavy lifting of fighting racism for years, began flooding in. How could I be silent and leave the emotional burden of educating my mostly white audience to people of color? Why wasn't I speaking out about my own racism and privilege? How could I support a system that threatened the health, well-being, and mental health of those I was purportedly helping? The comments were furious, and I was shocked and devastated as I read them.

The people I wanted to help didn't need, didn't want, and hadn't asked for a cow. They needed something else.

My ego immediately went into enthusiastic overdrive. How could people turn on ME, a supporter? Here I was trying to be an ally, exerting influence with my followers. I did exactly what was asked of me, and I'm the one getting schooled? Maybe that's why they don't get more help, they don't make it easy or pleasant, because I was damned if I did and damned if I didn't. I was so misunderstood!

Yeah. It wasn't pretty at first.

Thankfully, it occurred to me that I could follow the advice I had been dispensing to my fans and followers for years. If my goal was to help, I was getting clear instructions on what to do next. Here was an idea: I could bypass my chafed ego and stop personalizing the feedback. I had developed, and could use this opportunity to employ, a technique to stop ego spirals: Do the next thing that people I trusted were telling me to do. I could swallow my false pride and follow the simple instructions. It wasn't about me and my precious self-esteem. Here was a fresh opportunity to participate in my own undoing, because this was a deep and profound issue in which I had neither mastery nor expertise. I would stay involved, keep doing my best, even if it meant being confronted again and again about not doing it perfectly.

If I wanted to be an ally, and I did, I would look for the helpers, rely on the collective, soak up their feedback, reflect about my contributions to the problem, publicly narrate what I was learning, and document my own mistake-riddled journey.

SHE'S COME UNDONE

Years after our international adventure in Africa, my former roommate and I had a conversation during which she revealed insights she'd gained while doing transformative work at a retreat.

She realized that for too many years, she'd exerted control as a means of sidelining risk. But that practice came with a high cost. Asserting control, as in packing to avoid deprivation or discomfort, also meant less adventure and less learning. Though she had become an expert in her field and had great certainty about many things, she also often felt bored, lonely, and vulnerable. Her confidence in navigating a rapidly changing world was low. She worried about being replaced at work with new systems and becoming one of the "dinosaurs" that lumber through all workplaces.

At the retreat, she had begun working to remove her shield, replacing it with a desire to allow the world to impact her as much as she sought to impact the world. She wanted to come undone. I support her in that.

I am committed to becoming a lifelong unlearner. I am committed to letting myself be undone by the falling apart that continues to happen in my current life. I am committed to helping hope make a comeback.

I really believe we can emerge from hard times evolved instead of traumatized. My idealistic college student self continues on, convinced that together, we are genius. We can create better connections, a better workplace, and a better worldplace.

WAYS TO BUILD YOUR RESILIENCE

Among other things, resilience is the ability to emerge from difficult experiences or crises evolved instead of traumatized. Your chances of evolving will be enhanced by resisting the human tendency to argue with the current reality. Conserve your energy through acceptance, and steer clear of the tendency to wish reality were different or to desire to control the future.

Tend to the Basics

Double down on the habits and dedications that help you to move through the world as your best self. Commit to self-care, get great sleep, move your body, meditate to rest your mind, eat to fuel your journey.

Connect with Others

Dare to be vulnerable. Share how you are feeling without veering into venting. Ask others for help and ideas, and offer your own suggestions. Crowdsourcing strategies and information helps build a collective approach and eases the individual burden.

Dare to Try Something

Pause, and for the moment, radically simplify. Follow others' simple instructions as a place to begin. Be willing to try imperfect ideas or suggestions to give birth to discoveries. Sometimes the unadorned act of "making something work" begets innovation. Even if the solutions you develop are temporary, maybe even unsustainable, they can get you through to the next stages.

Question Everything

Reflect on what has been illuminated as valuable or detrimental. What has been revealed to you or about you? Where do you need to evolve next in order to skillfully walk through a changed world? From the place of simplification, question everything that you are tempted to add back to your life. Choose only that which is life-giving, not depleting. If you are struggling, consider three things: Are you willing to embrace a changing world, or are you pining for the past to return? Are you using outdated skill sets for a new reality? Are you using a less-than-modern approach in a new world?

Curate Your Life

Challenges and disruptions come with gifts. Do not waste them. Don't assume a predetermined outcome. Shift thinking away from "why we can't" or "why we shouldn't have to," and imagine a multitude of positive possibilities. Focus your efforts and choices in those directions.

QUESTION YOUR QUESTIONS

Should I stay, or should I go?

I'd been wrestling with the question for months, dragging around an anchor that didn't quite keep me in place but also didn't allow me to be free. My marriage felt too good to leave and too bad to stay.

This question, consequential and containing pain, traveled with me to Mount Kilimanjaro, a trek arranged by my husband for our family. Our group included my four sons, my husband, and one of his four sons. My husband had thoughtfully arranged the trip so that we would summit at Uhuru (Freedom) Peak on the Fourth of July, the day the U.S. celebrates independence.

Arriving at a summit called Freedom on a national day of independence had a symbolism to our relationship that did not escape me. Although I had scaled an epic peak, no revelation awaited me at the top. The answer to my stay-or-go question didn't appear in that thin air. But I did find a metaphor that would enable me, eventually, to achieve clarity that for so long eluded me.

Should I stay or should I go? I've been asked that question so often, by so many people. Should I stay in my job or leave? Should I continue this relationship or get out? Should I start my own business or stay put in my corporate role? Should I speak my mind or stay silent? Should I manage my children's decisions, or should I let them suffer the natural consequences?

That trip to Kilimanjaro helped me realize that the equation in this question is inherently flawed. The first problem is the word "should," which carries with it the heavy load of expectation and external influence, and the second is the word "or," which is a sucker's setup for duality thinking.

Once I returned from Kilimanjaro, I knew I had some serious soul-searching to do about a big life decision. To do it right, I would have to come up with much better questions.

TOO GOOD TO LEAVE

Author and philosopher Alain de Boton writes that "every fall into love involves the triumph of hope over self-knowledge. We fall in love hoping we won't find in another what we know is in ourselves."

That works for me.

I remember so clearly how sweetly it started, with romance, chemistry, and so much promise. Our relationship was born in fun and laughter and exotic trips together. He sang to me, and we danced in the kitchen. We both were bright and passionate, adventurous and fun-loving. I had four boys. He had four boys.

We had both been through difficult divorces and couldn't believe our good fortune to have found in each other a loyal, committed partner. We began to dream and scheme of the future we would build together. No more heartbreak for us!

I remember less clearly when the unraveling began, and even as I started to notice, I knew I played a part in the fraying. I had raced in, ignoring big stop signs along the way, confident that my big love and compromising nature could sustain us. When he was occasionally demanding, excluding me in decisions, hinting at a hard stop when I disagreed, I saw the leadership I thought I needed based upon expertise he asserted he had.

Eventually the fraying threatened to break the cord that connected us. Had I stopped loving him, had I stopped wanting to be with him, it would have been easy. But neither of those things were true, which made a go-or-stay decision feel impossible.

The trip to Kilimanjaro became a turning point.

I was undertrained for the hike, not quite ready for such a big undertaking. I settled in to the simple instructions of our guides, going slowly, step by step, pole by pole. No matter how long it took me to accomplish the day's hike, the guides were there with expertise and patient support.

My husband typically raced ahead with his son, thoroughly enjoying the experience and rarely checking in with me. As we reached the summit, me trailing behind, my sons were there waiting. They wanted us to do it together. My husband was missing—already on the summit and taking photos of this monumental experience with his son.

The image was striking. It was a microcosmic study of our relationship, a reality I desperately needed to see to help me decide my future. He was in his own world, enjoying the experience that he had planned and that I had provided for. During the hike, I felt in need of, and lacking, a partner. He left my sons to tend to me, and that felt familiar. My experience was that he left the hard things up to others to work out while he enjoyed the view.

As we descended, I became very sick with altitude poisoning. I had pushed too hard, stayed in the high altitude too long. The guides, increasingly concerned, decided I needed to get to a lower elevation more quickly. They put me on a stretcher and raced me to the next camp so my lungs could rebalance and recover. My boys trekked by my side. My husband, confident I'd be fine, continued on his own path. Some of the loneliness I felt in that moment I knew had been created by me. I was the woman who moved through the world pretending she had no needs. I had always surrounded myself with competent staff (and guides) and had raised caring boys who were devoted to their mom.

On our last day of descending the mountain, my husband raced ahead, beaming and bragging, proud to finish first. I was at the back of the pack, and it didn't escape my notice that we were no longer sharing this formidable journey together. My more leisurely pace allowed me to soak up the glorious forest, alternately welcoming light rain and then sunshine, which infused the dripping leaves with verdant light. My boys were slightly ahead, each taking turns hanging back from time to time to check in with me. It was a delight to see them ahead of me, sturdily moving forward, one foot in front of the other, connected as a band of brothers, laughing and eagerly anticipating the hot showers and good meals that awaited us. I imagined them walking into their future like that, independent yet connected.

I was mostly walking alone, except for a guide who appeared when I needed a little help traversing a treacherous gully. I had imagined my husband and I sharing this trip together in a different way. And even so, in that moment, I realized I was blissful, connected to myself, and confident about my future.

FREEDOM REDEFINED

When I reviewed my journals leading up to our time on Mount Kilimanjaro, I saw consistent themes of yearning for liberation and freedom that our trip eventually underscored. During the trek, I wore a necklace, which I had bought the year before, made from a liberty coin.

The revelation I had on that trip didn't immediately give me the answer that I was seeking. No stone tablet or burning bush. Instead, I felt a deep pull toward doing work that would help me get crystal clear about what I really wanted and needed. Freedom needed to be redefined and liberation fully reconsidered. Liberation and freedom from my husband wasn't what I yearned for; it was something more essential and elusive. I needed to leave the relationship, but I didn't want to leave him. And I wasn't sure how to figure it all out.

Often when I am doing deep questioning, I turn to poetry. Poets ask the universal questions in beautiful, elegant ways. Their questions have little do to with what you should do and everything to do with making decisions about who you want to be. A David Whyte poem helped me see my questions needed to change if I were to be clear about who I wanted to be in the world and how I wanted to feel while living.

A few lines in a single poem waltzed into my heart and continued to dance there, urging me to learn something essential and true: *"You must learn one thing. The world was made to be free in."* Freedom was at the core of my conflict, but maybe it wasn't about the marriage. I needed to find the space of internal freedom.

Should I stay or should I go? How could I know, for sure, that leaving a man I loved and risking a marriage I valued was heading in the best direction for the life I desired? I realized that focusing on the "right" decision was futile. In poetry, I had found a new guiding principle: *"Anything and anyone that does not bring you alive is too small for you."* The advice that followed was simple, illuminating the path to freedom: *"Give up all the other worlds except the one to which you belong."*

To which world did I belong? I began to ask deeper questions, and in answering those, I was led to a different kind of question altogether. My belief systems had kept me from rocking my marriage boat too hard. They had guided me to a crossroads where the world felt too small for me. What beliefs would I have to question to achieve my own freedom?

My husband and I had faced some really hard times together. We had both survived tough divorces and restored ourselves financially even in the wake of the financial crash of 2008. Our relationship had helped me heal in significant ways, and I believe I gave him those gifts as well. He understood independence was important to me. He encouraged me to keep my name, which was associated with the successful business I had created. He was fine with my travel schedule, which kept us apart for long periods of time. And if that sometimes felt lonely—no calling to check in that I arrived safely, no airport pickups, no dinners waiting when I arrived home from a long work trip—well, maybe that was the price to pay for "independence."

The way I saw it, our difficulties centered on three big issues: parenting and stepparenting, working in a business together with very different styles and backgrounds, and financial equity.

I had managed the first by purchasing a second home, just minutes from the one we had moved into together, so we could minimize conflict, maintain domestic tranquility, and parent our sons in our own distinctive ways.

In business, our differing styles and approaches had created turmoil among the team, so I carved out a piece of my business for him, allowing him to work from home, set his own destiny, and contribute financially in a different way.

Resolution of the third issue eluded us. As we hit some rough waters, I could see we might have overestimated our abilities. I couldn't solve this on my own. I needed something from him as well, but he protected his newfound interests. The value equation in our relationship kept getting worse. From my perspective, he began showing up less, delivering minimally, procrastinating family and work duties as I frantically worked harder to keep the dream alive. He seemed stalled in his growth. The drama of it all skyrocketed.

I had done so much compromising that I was becoming confused about who I was. I ignored the ringing of the temple bells. I fell asleep. When the yearning for the impossible dream became overwhelming, I numbed myself with more work and too much alcohol. I mislaid my voice and lost my way. I became a little girl again.

And now I was twirling in the should-I-stay-should-I-go question. Which, as we have established, was the wrong question.

FINDING THE QUESTIONS

I decided to do my own work without worrying whether my husband was doing his.

From post-Kilimanjaro July to October, I began asking the harder internal questions and examining my belief systems.

I'd gotten stuck in the good/bad trap. When I asked the "Should I" question, I became ambivalent. The calculation became situational, and therefore the answer constantly changed. When we had a great weekend, and I felt connected and close, I thought I should stay. Other times, when an attempt at communication turned into a lecture and left me feeling humiliated, well, screw that. I should leave! The cycle was crazy making.

I needed questions that would take me out of duality thinking (right/wrong, good/bad, desirable/undesirable), that would transcend ego. So I began searching for the ones that would instantly expand my possibilities.

What if the question was this: Was I fulfilled?

To answer that, I needed to stop obfuscating my reality. My preference was to live out my life with this man I dearly loved. But if I were honest about the current reality of our marriage, I was not fulfilled. I knew I was living smaller than I could be.

Another question appeared: What did my soul crave? I was a little heartsick as I realized I had known the answer to this for a long time. I craved freedom and independence within a marriage to a man I dearly loved. I had exhausted myself by crawling up to the edge of asking, even demanding, what I needed within the container of our relationship. But I wouldn't quite knock down the wall with supreme clarity, by boldly stating my needs.

Here was a juicy question: What was I afraid of? If I was clear, what kept me from just asking for what I needed? What was I believing that kept me in fear?

I was afraid of being seen as a quitter. I had made a commitment. I have integrity.

I didn't want to have failed in a second marriage—what would people think? Standing up for myself would reinforce his belief that I am only about the money.

I'd been working so damn hard to make it work. Shouldn't I continue? And then more revealing questions came to me: What if the choice was between staying in the marriage or abandoning myself? What if divorce was an act of integrity?

The expansive questions continued to emerge: Was I willing to let people be wrong about me in order to find personal fulfillment and happiness? Was I willing to give up the dream of the life I thought I'd signed up for in order to find the life I needed to live?

As I got closer to clarity, my ego weighed in with this scary question: What if this is my one and only chance at big love? I had the sense to examine that for truth and discarded the premise of the question. It implied I have no part in filling my life with big love. Love doesn't find you by chance. I had the power to create it. How I lived and loved was up to me.

Was I willing to give up perfection for the good? And was I willing to shed my image as a "good girl" so that I could more fully be a wholehearted woman, a woman who was true to herself? What if I focused less on how not to be wrong in others' eyes and more on how to be right in my own?

The final question appeared: Did I really have the courage to remove all the barriers to living the life of which I dreamed?

In the midst of all this questioning, I found myself alone, at a very challenging time, a fresh empty nester. My business was threatened, and I had serious health challenges knocking at my door. A world health crisis had erupted, and my best friend was dying.

After three months of reflecting, listening to podcasts, meditating, filling my bookshelves with books on creating healthy relationships, journaling, and googling "how to know when it is time to go" (yeah, I admit it), my truth was revealed: I love my husband. I wanted to be with him. But for that to be, he had to be willing to honor my boundaries.

I didn't want to be alone, yet my definition of freedom was not "being allowed to come and go as I pleased." I wanted to be free to think independently. I wanted the independence of owning what I had created without being forced to merge it all into our marriage to prove my love. I wanted to choose who got the rewards of what I created without his demands or supervision or control. I wanted the liberation of owning my own soul without owing anyone for that privilege and right. Any time I stepped out to be free, I was threatened with abandonment. It was a conundrum: I gave up my freedom to be loved, but freedom was what I needed in order to love.

I wanted to fully join the man I loved only as an equal partner. No longer was I willing to pay a ransom for what was already mine. As Mary Oliver, another of my favorite poets, said, "There is only one life to save, and that is your own."

I would extend an invitation for a relationship reset, to establish the things that were clearly mine in the name of equity and fairness. I would place my bet on a second chance for us to create a love all the sweeter for having worked it through.

Although I really dislike hurting others, I also know that doing what's right for me risks hurting others. Speaking my truth came with the risk of rejection. But I also thought I knew my husband. He had always been committed to working things through with others he had loved. Surely he would do the same for me, the woman he called the love of his life.

Smiling, with a joyful heart, relieved, and hopeful, I set out to prepare for a different conversation with my beloved.

THE GREAT LETTING GO

With my newfound clarity, much of the fear of what might happen fell away. What would happen wasn't for me to decide. I had created this wonderful life, and I could create a different wonderful life. I stopped seeing this relationship as my only chance to be loved. That was like saying I had no power to co-create my future. My definition of integrity shifted. I would be true to myself.

"Soulmate" took on a different meaning—not the person you would be with forever but rather someone who would change you forever for having known them. A soulmate was someone who came into your life to teach you a soul lesson, a big thing you need to know. I needed to know how to advocate for myself, to stand up for what is mine, and to be brave enough to live my big purpose.

The truth was, we had been dancing around this third issue for four years. My annual New Year's intention setting, for four years in a row, had centered on feeling alive again: centered, creative, tuned in, wide awake, and less exhausted. I'd been asking timidly. He had dodged and feinted, and I had ducked and covered. In reality, I revisited this issue to the point of embarrassing myself, and no matter what his words were, the answer in his actions had always been no. I hadn't wanted to see it.

My vision of our future was so clear. I would be free to love him without requirement and without resentments. I could see a big beautiful future—slowing down, enjoying time at the ocean in a new home, learning, traveling together on grand adventures, kids raised, finally together under one roof. He would fully engage his life's work instead of focusing on mine and overinvolving himself in my legacy. I would be free at last, and I could feel the excitement of a love fueled by personal growth and evolution.

I decided to extend the invitation one more time, with confidence and clarity and consequence, and pay close attention to the answer.

The universe itself will provide answers if your questions are pure and from the heart, when you are focused on living your potential instead of working to reconstruct your reality. I would state my needs, cleanly and clearly, and accept the final answer. As the poet Rilke says, "When you can trust yourself, you will know how to live." When you are aligned with yourself and speak your truth, that which is true and those who are meant for you will remain, and the rest will fall away.

"I love you and want to be together. This is what I need to be me and to feel free in our marriage."

And just like that, the marriage fell away.

Step by step, pole by pole, I have picked up the pieces and tended to the details of my life, putting in order each part. I am enjoying my freedom and definitely feel liberated as I plan for the next life I will love.

I am enjoying the solo walk in a metaphorical sunlit rainforest, watching my boys move into their future as I co-create my own.

HOW TO CHANGE YOUR QUESTIONS

It's normal to feel frozen in indecision when you're trying to find the exact path or the steps that will lead to your desired life. Who doesn't want the prediction of a crystal ball or a wise inner voice to whisper the secret formula that will move you forward and deliver more happiness?

That is magical thinking, and life doesn't work that way. I don't really have to tell you that, but I will say that when you feel unsure of how to go forward, it's time to go inward.

In my master's degree program, I would get so frustrated when my quickly formed research questions, which were based on minimal reflection, were rejected by my professors over and over again. They steadfastly insisted I invest meaningful effort into posing a great question that would produce a satisfactory payoff. The right question, they maintained, would make the research easier and produce clearer insights. They were right. For months, I struggled with finding "the question," and once it was perfected, the research it led to produced mind-blowing discoveries that, twenty years later, would form the basis of my career.

If you want better answers, start with better questions. Begin by writing down the question that continually appears in your mind—the one question that feels necessary to answer in order to act.

When you are going in circles trying to find answers, here are ways to help you find a better question.

Check for the Word "Should"

Framing a question in terms of "should" is a product of conditioning and is likely to land you in a no-win situation. "Should" signals that there is one right thing to do and will likely lead you to focus externally, looking for ways to measure up to what others expect or need from you. "Should" leads you to outsource your happiness.

Watch Out for the Word "Or"

It's a setup and leads to the sucker's choice. It promotes duality thinking, where choices are limited, extreme, and often unfulfilling and painful. Reality—living happy in the mess—calls you to reject "or" so you can see the whole spectrum of possibilities and choices. The "good/bad" trap that springs from the word "or" promotes ambivalence and indecisiveness. Because the calculation becomes situational, it constantly changes.

Direct Your Focus Inward

When your question (and answer) is anchored in the external world, which is ever-changing, you need big questions to open up your mind and connect you with your heart's desire. Here are two great questions to try on for size:

1. Am I currently fulfilled?

2. What is my soul craving?

These big questions require reflection, and time and space. You must walk with them over time. The answer won't come from your intellect but rather from your inner knowing. Be patient even when it feels urgent; the immediate answers may evade you, as if the muse who carries them is shy after being silenced for so long.

Look Around You for Clues

The answer you're seeking is more like the "gold" found after a treasure hunt, not a score that comes from a Google quiz. When I allowed myself to experience my home surroundings as a curious observer, I found many big clues.

My bookcases were filled with books on how to make marriage more fulfilling—his were not. I had given him one book, I can still see the beautiful red cover, with an invitation for a personal "book club" so we could talk about it together. It lay unopened, my loving inscription inside unread, on the nightstand.

I saw the inspirational quotes hung on my mirror about being free and loving big. Right below it lay the necklace I bought late one night and had worn for most of the year, fashioned from a liberty coin. Sometimes looking objectively at your surroundings provides clues that can help you find an answer you have known but haven't wanted or been able to see.

You don't have to delve deep, just look for themes. Check your journals and other pieces of writing. When I began seeing the words "liberation" and "freedom" in four years of New Year's resolutions, I finally realized I needed to pay attention. As a lover of poetry, I noticed that, too, helped me to know my answer. "Anything that does not bring you alive is too small for you." I was stopped in my tracks every time I heard or read that poem by David Whyte. Check out your own songs, poetry, movie lines, or social media posts. Ask yourself what lines resonate with you, bring you to tears. What have you returned to over and over again when you are feeling despair?

Once you hear the whispered or shouted answer of whether you are fulfilled, once your soul has revealed its craving, work to give yourself that. Ask for what you need cleanly and lovingly and directly. If you find yourself unable, if that scares the breath out of you—this is a sign that you are involved in deep healing work for yourself. Commit to one more round of questions: What are you believing that fuels the fear? What stops you from asking for what your soul craves?

This is big, so get it down on paper. Write your fears and your limiting beliefs, and question those beliefs. This endeavor will lead to more soul searching and even better questions. I was afraid of being alone. I feared I was unlovable unless I paid the tributes demanded by others. I worried that this relationship was my only chance at love. I dreaded being seen as greedy or a quitter or a fraud. Basically, I feared what others might think of me.

Once you bring your fears to light, they begin to fall away. Once you question your limited beliefs, you can choose to live by what is true for you. Perhaps then you will be ready to ask for what you desire. No begging, no justifying, just the ask.

See Reality as It Is

After that comes your toughest work. Believe the answer that comes. Trust it. Take it at face value. If the answer is aligned with your craving and your hopes, rejoice! Celebrate, and thank those involved for their beautiful gift of love and generosity. Try to live up to that new state of largeness.

If the answer is other than what you hoped, settle into the grief of knowing. Then summon up gratitude for finally having clarity. Grieve until you can rejoice, celebrate, and thank those involved for their beautiful gift of love and honesty. Live up to that new state of largeness.

AMENDS

In one of the most desperate situations of my young adult life, I reached out to my dad for unconditional love, support, and a safe place to land. I needed a dad who had my back, who would take me in and help me straighten out my life. But in that moment, he chose to be a judge, a moral instructor, and a disciplinarian. In essence, he turned me away with an age-old finger-wagging platitude: "You made your bed. Time to lie in it."

In the end, I found a way to clean up my own mess, and in doing so, I learned a lot about myself and life while living in a tent by a lake for an entire summer. Maybe he thought he had done me a favor, but throughout my recovery, I didn't forgive, and I wouldn't forget. For months I stayed incommunicado, leaving him to wonder where I was and what I was doing. I felt done with my dad.

After I got back into college and fell in love, I went home to visit, hesitant and nervous, because my boyfriend wanted to ask for my hand in marriage. My dad didn't know much about my life at that point or what to expect during our visit. I hadn't prepped him much. After my fiancé told Dad he wanted to marry me, my dad sarcastically said he'd be glad to have me off his hands. He offered to pay for us to elope, which would spare him the expense of the big weddings my two sisters had enjoyed. I was wounded by his response to what was, for me, an epic life moment. My simmer became a boil, and I swore to myself I would never ask him for anything again. He would be invited to my wedding, but only as a guest in a tuxedo. I broke our family tradition—and let go of my lifelong dream—by not asking him to walk me down the aisle. I wanted to hurt him as much as he had hurt me.

On what was supposed to be one of the happiest days of my life, I felt so much shame knowing I had cheated myself out of fully sharing that day with my dad. I cried all through the father-daughter dance—the last dance we would have together. Dancing with my dad had always been special. My parents were terrific dancers. On Sunday afternoons, Dad would turn on the music, and the kids would line up by age and wait for our turn for him to teach us the steps.

Our messy, complicated relationship continued after I married. My dad could be preachy and insensitive and stubborn, and then he would confuse me with tenderness. I began to see him as an iron-clad marshmallow, and I wondered what the iron armor was meant to protect. He had faced so much heartbreak and disappointment throughout his own life. I started to soften. I missed him and wanted him back in my life, but I couldn't see how to make it happen.

When I was expecting my second son, I was on bedrest for

LIFE'S MESSY, LIVE HAPPY

much of the pregnancy. Although I was pregnant with twin boys, the underdeveloped twin absorbed back into my placenta, causing bleeding and premature labor. My husband and I had endured months of fertility treatments, and after everything we'd been through, the baby who kept growing felt like a miracle.

I had a lot of time to think during this confinement. My dad had three sets of twins in his family, and I wanted to name this singular twin after my dad. At the same time, I didn't see how I could honor him that way when our relationship was so unresolved. I was still stuck in shame over my wedding. He'd had a stroke, and though he'd recovered, I was worried about losing him.

During my bedrest, I spent weeks reflecting on my contributions, sorting through some of the awful things I had done, trying to bat away justifications for my choices because, in my view, he'd been horrid. I had thought, "He is the adult! He should be the one to apologize to me for all the things he's done! He should have taken care of me." And then I realized I was on the cusp of thirty years old and expecting my second baby. I also was an adult. Perhaps my righteous advice for him was a simple instruction for myself: make amends.

I crafted a clean apology. I spent days processing and rehearsing and role-playing. I swore that no matter how he responded, I wouldn't allow him to derail me from this major relationship-repair attempt. Once I was off bedrest, I went to see him.

Not asking him to walk me down the aisle as a means of retaliation was the greatest regret of my life, I told him. I had personalized his sarcastic humor with hurt and fear that sprang from desperately wanting to feel loved and respected. I acknowledged the great pain I had caused him with some of my life choices. I thanked him for doing his best as a father and asked him to consider forgiving me. And whether he forgave me or not, I wanted him to know my ultimate amends would be to name my second son after him: Charles O'Larry, who I hoped would have the best qualities of his grandfather.

It wasn't all angel choruses and sunlight breaking through dark clouds. He cracked a few jokes flavored with his characteristic sarcasm. ("I know it was tough on you, but it made you stronger. Look how you turned out," he said.) But I didn't take the bait. I looked past his armor and waited. As we continued talking, he spoke more of his truth. He was so happy to see me. He was proud of who I had become. He felt relieved that life brought second chances. Two miracles had happened: my second son survived, and our relationship was restored. We wept together.

My intention had been to give him forgiveness, and even though he never apologized to me, the reconciliation I received was equally precious. Dad barely remembered the details of events that I had clung to for years. With my apology, I healed what seemed like generations of damage caused by parenting with too much discipline and not enough demonstrative love. Our conversation seemed to ease his fears and worries and regrets. I was almost thirty years old, and it was the first time I felt truly close to him.

We got a relationship reset, a father and a daughter, two adults. I enjoyed our visits and made them more frequently. I sorted through what had been given to me, discarding what wasn't useful and feeling grateful for what was. He had taught me hard work, pride in my name and reputation, and a passion for making the world a better place. The example of how he lived made me brave enough to speak my truth and to stand up for what I believe. The sudden shift of perception from fear to love that my apology inspired showed me that even when deep relationship hurts happen, small moments of mercy and grace can erase years of resentment.

From that time forward, he showed up for me. I asked for him, and I allowed what he would offer, even if it was imperfect. He was at Charles O'Larry Wakeman's baptism. He was integral in helping us make a dream come true as we restored our beautiful historic home. He did what was seemingly impossible—using his meticulous craftsman skills to move a one-hundred-year-old carriage house to a new location to make room for our family pool. He was there for me the night my mother died and to break the news of my brother Tim's death. When my husband broke his neck, he showed up to take the kids.

I gave birth to an apology right before I gave birth to my dad's namesake. Two intertwined blessings. That apology gave me my dad back, the dad I had always wanted.

THE GIFT IN AN APOLOGY

Not all apologies produce those kinds of miracles. But apologies coupled with amends are important. The fact is, you can't be responsible for how other people feel about or respond to your words and actions. Even so, owning the actions that cause hurt and offering a sincere "I am sorry" go a long way toward helping you live happily in the mess. The fine art of delivering an apology is an essential life skill for adults, yet another path to freedom.

An apology, and making amends, is something you do for you. It's a way to acknowledge your guilt while releasing your shame. It's a gesture of goodwill that demonstrates you want to repair a relationship and clear the clutter of your conscience. You gift yourself.

Recipients of an apology can choose to seize the opportunity to heal from the hurt and harm they felt and open themselves to the possibility of forgiveness. A clean apology can provide profound relief. It can stop the obsessive downward spiral of trying to figure out what the hell happened and why you did what you did. It frees others up to direct energy toward their own healing.

Whether they actually do that—forgive and heal—isn't your business. True amends means releasing that need. When you apologize, forgiveness is neither guaranteed nor deserved—that is the other person's privilege and work. Keep that in mind when someone apologizes to you. Your healing, and your ability to forgive, is your work.

I once was on the receiving side of a wonderful, flawless apology. A colleague with whom I shared a professional background, whom I'll call Susan, became a dear friend as we discovered we had a lot in common. She was talented and honest and caring. I invited her along on a retreat-like work trip with my team. During that trip, behind the scenes and without my knowledge, she helped fuel drama that was swirling among members of the team. Susan entertained long venting sessions and counseled an employee who had issues with me. Her coaching did eventually prompt the employee to come to me for a conversation, but the distraction and drama continued throughout the trip. Susan and the employee spent hours away from the rest of us. They were distant when the team was together. In the end, what I had intended to be a pleasurable, bonding retreat for my team and my friend turned into a miserable experience for everyone.

I felt she had betrayed my confidences and our friendship. Getting involved with my employee violated boundaries and crossed ethical lines. Susan admitted that she had allowed herself to be manipulated by a charismatic employee. After I discovered she had been involved for months, even taking that employee on as a coaching client, I was furious. She had violated my trust, created a conflict of interest in her own practice, and fueled behavior that damaged my team's morale. I expressed my disappointment and betrayal and discontinued the friendship.

After many months, Susan reached out and asked to talk, but I had set a boundary. I chose not to respond. One day in a grocery store, we bumped into each other. The surprise encounter gave her an opportunity to apologize. She said she was sorry and acknowledged that her actions had been wrong. She conceded she had overestimated her skills for managing the situation. Overconfidence, even arrogance, had led her to think she could facilitate a resolution to the conflict. She admitted she'd sailed into a kind of turbulence she didn't have the tools to navigate. Her reflections made her aware this was a pattern in her life. She didn't like that aspect of herself, she said, and was working on a course correction. She asked what she could do to make it up to me.

Even the conclusion to the apology was flawless. She didn't ask for an immediate reply. Susan told me she didn't expect anything, although she hoped we could find our way back to being friends. She gave me space and respected my boundaries. At the time, I forgave what felt authentic—I can empathize with overstepping in the name of help—but it didn't immediately restore the relationship. I needed more time.

After attending a party at my house, Susan made a second apology in a sweet note left behind in my home. Her apology healed a hurt that had been festering for a long time. Still, I chose not to resume the friendship in the same way. Though I forgave her, I can't say it was 100 percent. I forgave enough so that resentment about what happened between us doesn't hurt me, and I respected my need to trust completely the people I allow in my inner circle.

It's not that I don't have compassion for her or appreciate the vulnerability she showed in apologizing so sincerely. I am grateful. Anyone who knows me even a little knows I screw up all the time. However, my view is that an apology isn't a transaction that comes with a 100 percent forgiveness guarantee. I chose to hang on to a small percentage of unforgiveness as a reminder to create boundaries around sharing deeply private information about my life. I hang on not to the hurt but to the memory of what can happen when I overshare.

ENTER THE EGO

The ego has a big role to play in both conflict and crafting an apology. The ego will try to co-opt the apology to get what it wants: some kind of vindication. This happened to me many years ago. A close friend and I were at a work party, visiting and joking around, when our boss approached us. After greeting him, she began giving him what I saw as way too much information about what we'd been discussing, including a description of my views. I felt like she was showing off AND throwing me under the bus. I found the conversation so upsetting that I left the party.

The next day, as was our routine, she invited me to grab a cup of coffee. When I showed up, I laid into her. I assigned bad motives to what she'd said at the party and brought up some of her past transgressions for good measure. I threatened to reveal things she'd shared with me. I said unkind things. Then I escalated the drama by storming out of the coffee shop.

My next move was to pout and shut her out. I chose to exclude her from a couple of important meetings. She responded with her own acts of aggression. As I nursed my wounds over several weeks, reinforced by my ego-based stories, I began to wonder who I was punishing. I missed her. Honestly, our interaction hadn't been my finest moment. I could see my contributions to our continued conflict, and my heart opened. I wanted "us" back. Time to apologize. I asked if we could get together for a conversation.

My insecurities and discomfort around a boss I'd been trying to impress had triggered bad behavior, I told her, and I was so sorry. I let my competitive spirit get the best of me, I confessed. After the party, I had trapped myself in ego-based stories without examining whether they were true. I had come to our post-party coffee meeting not to make up but to take a righteous stand. I committed to taking more risks and talking things out before they swelled into an entire body of pain. My apology was honest and sincere. I made myself vulnerable and accountable.

I finished, and I waited. And waited. I had an expectation that a similar apology would be forthcoming. Where was the grand confession about *her* part in the conflict? I had given her the space to admit the ways she had tried to humiliate me and to reveal how she went out of her way to one-up me in front of our bosses.

Silence. Apparently, she saw no need to apologize.

I got angry all over again. I reaccused her of the same things, in the same way, with a full display of the behavior that I had just apologized for!

My ego had co-opted my apology. With additional reflection, I realized my intention had been underhanded. While I wanted to be relieved of the guilt and shame of my bad behavior, my apology also was a manipulative attempt to get her to own her part in the conflict and apologize so we could be on equal footing again. That damn ego had pulled me into its trap again.

More reflection helped me see that my motives were way less than pure. Eventually, I crafted a more wholehearted apology, which included apologizing for my previous apology. Whew. At last, I felt the relief I'd been seeking.

TRY, TRY AGAIN . . . THEN LET GO

Sometimes it takes more than one apology go-around to make things right. Done right, apology and amends have the potential to restore trust and strengthen the relationship. You've demonstrated it can survive hard times!

However, keep in mind that "making things right" doesn't necessarily come with a requirement to restore a relationship with someone else. While apologies may open the door to a fresh start, the main benefit is an improved or restored relationship with yourself. That means you'll need to do the personal work that leads to internal healing, the most fulfilling benefit of a sincere, heartfelt apology.

In harming another, you feel two feelings: guilt, which is healthy, and shame, which is unhealthy. Healthy guilt reminds you that you weren't true to your convictions or values and inspires you to improve. Shame is just the pile on, in which you add the story of how you are not enough and will never be enough.

If you're skipping apologies and amends, you're forgoing the inner work necessary to heal yourself. It will leave a film on your soul—a film of shame. The accumulation of shame dims your light and keeps you stuck in a vicious cycle of bad behavior and more shame.

Self-reproach is a burden from the past that you carry into the present, another tool with which to beat yourself up. Vulnerability, the prerequisite of courage, accelerates internal processing and personal healing. You examine your actions, keep what is yours, get insight into your triggers, and forgive yourself. Deep reflection and self-forgiveness are the ultimate shame reducers. Once you're clear, you speak of your guilt, with transparency and vulnerability, in the light of day. An apology acknowledges the (healthy) guilt and replaces (unhealthy) shame with acceptance. Making amends, committing to changes in behavior no matter how imperfect, restores your ability to trust yourself to be more of who you really are, not who your shame and ego would have you believe.

Wholehearted attempts at amends, actual changes in behavior, are essential. The bigger the apology, the more inner work you need to do. You're shouldering a big responsibility to not layer harm on top of past harm. Continually betraying trust by committing additional acts of harm is manipulative and cruel— even abusive.

Don't apologize for big things lightly. You're issuing a powerful invitation for another person to facilitate healing by doing their own work, so it's imperative to be clear and honest about your intentions.

In the course of writing this book, I received the sweet surprise of a beautiful, heartfelt apology, with revelations of vulnerability, insight, and deep remorse for the actions that I felt wounded by. It was a gilt-edged invitation to conscious forgiveness, and I took it seriously. I committed to doing the deep work required of me to achieve that. I read books, got into therapy, took courses, completed worksheets. I even curated my Instagram account to facilitate my healing and hasten forgiveness.

I met the apology with an open heart and hard work because I wanted to restore the relationship with total forgiveness. A few months after that oh-so-beautiful apology, the person began to redefine his amends—the promised change in behavior. Apparently, the apology had dissipated his guilt and settled our dispute. Once he felt that relief, his commitment to do the deep work required to restore trust and redefine our relationship began shifting. He found reason after reason for not following through with the promised amends.

In the end, I got great benefit out of doing my own work, and I don't regret it. Even so, the broken promise made me realize the reconnection I so longed for could never happen, which was deeply painful. The experience strengthened my resolve to only offer amends I was committed to and could follow through on.

Be careful with your amends—making promises you either don't intend to keep or aren't sure that you can deliver on is among the cruelest things you can do to another. Asking someone to make themselves vulnerable enough to trust you again, then following that up with additional disappointment or betrayal is irresponsible at minimum and causes reckless harm. That's why it's so important to be crystal clear about your real intentions and your willingness to do the work it would take to fulfill the promise of change. That is the heart and soul of an authentic apology. Healing and forgiveness are a precious, fragile gift. Hold them in your hands and heart like you would a wounded bird. If you can't live up to your promise, don't make it.

When apologies don't go well, it's fine to try again. Thank heavens my work colleague gave me a second chance. But when it's clear that delivered apologies aren't accompanied by the wholehearted attempts to change the relationship dynamics that caused harm, letting go might be the healthiest thing you can do. You might just need to step away. I've adopted an informal rule: attempt three times, in three different ways, and if it keeps going sideways, let go. Don't get trapped into a familiar toxic dance. An apology doesn't need to turn into groveling or being held captive to someone else's ego-based stories.

In one instance, my attempts at apology and forgiveness of someone I loved deeply only exacerbated the emotional conflict in which we were embroiled. He had betrayed me, and I had wounded him.

I tried to apologize several times, in different ways, only to have the apology critiqued, criticized, and judged as inadequate. When I tried to describe my experience, he dismissed it as inaccurate, because he didn't remember things the way I did. He was interruptive. His efforts to control and script my apology felt like an attempt to heal injuries far beyond what I had done or caused, and in the end, he denied himself the very thing that he craved—acknowledgment of my wrongs, validation that it wasn't about him, that he was a good person who gave me many gifts. There was no apology that could have been perfect enough, because what he needed was beyond my ability to repair.

I wanted to be settled, but after so many attempts, I decided to end the dance and settle myself. The apology I had hoped would be accepted remains undelivered. And in my mind, undeliverable.

A wrong done in the present can trigger a recall of all the times someone has been hurt in the past, and when that happens, it's important to realize that sometimes another's wounds aren't yours to heal. Even so, it doesn't mean the apology is not worth doing.

I've made peace with the fact that the only way I could make amends in that situation was to forgive this man and myself. My amends will be made by living differently in future relationships, where I intend to work hard not to make the same kinds of errors. Maybe the person I hurt directly won't benefit, but if I can heal by forgiving myself and letting go, others will become the beneficiaries of lessons learned.

The experience has reinforced my commitment to work hard

at accepting apologies, no matter how imperfect. I want to lean in to the vulnerability and generosity of that simple act. Even a poor attempt to repair is a bold attempt. Insisting on perfection is a form of punishment, the ego's way of seeking intellectual relief and avoiding vulnerability. Your wounds, another's wounds, are always going to be bigger than the act being apologized for, and in that sense, it's your work to heal yourself. Hear the apology, and make your own choices about forgiveness and reconciliation. Learning to let go can be a different and equally valid form of restoration and renewal.

Of course, not every apology has to be elaborate. Depending on your actions, it can be one sentence that covers the bases. I am sorry, I acknowledge this affected you, I have insight, and I want to get back to things being right with us.

Making frequent apologies keeps your slate clean and your self-reflection skills sharp. Try to notice where your actions are fueled by fear rather than love. It's good information to have if you're working on being happy in the mess. And accept the apologies of others, even if they're imperfect. Be present, lean in, listen intently. You just need to receive the apology—the processing, healing, and forgiveness can come in your own time. You can decide what is true for you and set boundaries accordingly.

The inner work of self-reflection is essential. Owning, grieving, shifting perceptions, releasing—doing these things makes room for a potential miracle, in the moment or in time.

Self-reflection married to apology is where the magic happens. At least, that has typically been true for me. It gave me my dad back.

THE ELEMENTS OF APOLOGY

Apologies and amends are a bold step toward personal account-ability, releasing shame and pain, and laying the foundation for moving forward in a positive way.

If you've behaved in a way that puts a relationship at risk, you've likely toggled into low self. Accountability and apology is an antidote for the guilt and shame that can fuel future bad behavior.

The true work of a great apology is done in self-reflection. Stay in self-reflection until you feel clear and clean enough to deliver an apology with the following four components:

1. Name specifically what you did that left another feeling harmed or diminished—even if you didn't do it on purpose. Say the words "I am sorry." Define the specific words or behavior while shedding residual justification or blaming the other. Don't wallow in shame—just acknowledge where you missed the mark. Owning bad behavior doesn't indict you as a person. For example, "I am sorry. I jumped to conclusions, raised my voice, and left the room before the conversation was done. That wasn't appropriate, nor is it how I want to behave. I just want you to know that I'm sorry."

2. Acknowledge the effect your words or behavior had on another. It doesn't mean you caused them to behave badly, it's a statement of your actions that caused pain or doubt or hurt or some other tangible, harmful outcome. Demonstrate empathy for how

your actions must have made the other person feel. "I want to acknowledge that I hurt you, and I'm so sorry. My attempt at humor left you feeling diminished. My sarcasm had you second-guessing yourself and questioning my commitment to you."

3. Share insights—not excuses—that demonstrate self-reflection and increased self-knowledge about what might have prompted you to say or do what you did. This establishes that you understand what drove your behavior, that you don't blame the other person, and that you want to change. "I realized I was scared, and I often use righteousness and sarcasm and snarkiness when I feel that way. We were trying to sort out something important to you, and I became afraid you were doubting our relationship. I feel bad about it, and I am sorry."

4. Make amends—no sincere apology is complete without behavior change. The amends is a stated intention to change or improve your behavior going forward. Ask the question "How can I make this right with you?" The commitment should be realistic. Maybe not "I'll never do that again" but rather "I'm willing to work on this so it doesn't happen again in the future." And make good on the commitment by doing the personal work to change your behavior.

PART THREE

LOVE WINS

A LETTER TO MY SON

Dear Son:

You asked if I believe in a Higher Power. I haven't shared much about that with you. I am private, and I have not wanted to press my beliefs on you. But as you are searching, and because you asked, I realize that my experience might be helpful. I would love to engage in a lifelong dialogue on this topic. We might never figure it out, but wouldn't it be wonderful to try?

A Higher Power doesn't need to be found or figured out—it will find you. All you have to do is open your heart and your mind. Your Higher Power will find you in the great feedback you get from a friend, a mental or emotional breakthrough, the miracle of seeing something from a new angle, the feeling of being loved when you were convinced you were unlovable. The feeling is small at first. When you feel it, it is as though you are waking up to a whole new world, seeing more clearly with a different set of eyes, a life-saving, thirst-quenching shift in perspective. You start to understand your future is unbounded and all things are possible. You discover the hidden door to a better way, where everyone is on your side, and the kind universe is working in your favor, for your highest good.

You might notice that life leads you where you need to go and gives you just what you need in the nick of time. You notice that circumstances, even some that don't seem so great at the time, work out in your favor. You feel there is a guardian angel in your life who protects you against all odds. You feel grace and others' mercy. You see that people forgave you, that you were saved in spite of yourself, that you were led to the right people who gave you the right message at just the right time. You have run into the power of something bigger when you realize that things aren't as bad as you thought and people are more accepting than you could have imagined. Others have been where you have been, and they understand.

Trust those first signs. Open up to the early inklings. Notice the coincidences, signs, symbols, hawks, the weird, and the unexplainable. These are your first wake-up calls that something bigger is going on. A Higher Power is the ultimate arranger of coincidence.

When you get unexpected breakthroughs, these amazing chances at greatness, consider them preordained. When you are given opportunities that exceed your wildest expectations, and your life is swept away from you, you'll realize you are no longer in charge. Great fortune shows up and demands your presence.

You stop seeking and start accepting, following simple

instructions. You choose to trust that where you are led is exactly where you need to go. You settle in and begin to see the miracles everywhere. If you can surrender and acknowledge that something expansive and wise is in charge, suddenly life gets simpler. All you have to do on any given day is love the person in front of you, ease the suffering you see, feed the hungry person, share your experience with those who are just beginning.

Accept all feeding of your soul, no matter who the chef is. Master the lessons you are given. Surrender early and often.

A Higher Power allows you to bypass the fight and the fury and settle in quickly, conserving your energy by accepting what is and loving what is. What you might not yet know is that your Higher Power is way ahead of you. It has already performed great miracles for you, and you are the last to know. You will always be catching up to what is already perfect and as it should be. You are the last to see the amazing grace.

Why? I think the knowing is too big in the beginning, and we are allowed only glimpses so that we won't be afraid. The Higher Power is kind, it stays hidden and reveals itself slowly because if you knew the total glory of it all, you might decide you are unworthy. Seeing our own perfection and amazing glory all at once, especially when our ego is convinced we are undeserving, might scare us off. God is revealed in tiny pieces, like a trail of bread crumbs, to get you intrigued and keep you unafraid.

You might sometimes think it would be better if the Higher Power just revealed itself once and for all, super quick and full on, but your Higher Power knows you well. Rather than

throwing you off the dock into the water to experience that
numbing, cold shock, it wakes you up gently with a loving call
and a few snooze alarms. The light is dim in the beginning,
before the shower of full brightness.

In the beginning, it is so hard to believe that there isn't
some catch to the whole deal. How can a Higher Power be
so kind, so easygoing? We don't believe partly because we
haven't always seen the many examples of the Higher Power in
action here on earth. We get jaded, a bit blind to it all. We start
believing the crazy story that something is wrong with us and
with the world.

But eventually you will start noticing the Higher Power
everywhere, like when you say just the right thing in a moment
when you couldn't have known the right thing to say. Suddenly
it feels like the top of your head opens up, and spirit inspires you
to say something profound. You get to be the messenger because
you are open to being God-inspired. Maybe your words alter the
path of another, and you are amazed. You can't imagine where
that came from because it was a thought you never thought
before. You were a vessel. You were taught just in time. In that
moment, you glimpse the reality of a Higher Power.

I know the Higher Power even if I can't name it. It is the
ideal me, it gives me the strength to get through hard things
like your dad's accident, the deaths of my mom and dad and
your uncle Tim. It gives me the courage to write down my
thoughts in books, the guts to speak my truth, the urge to
get up after I have failed. It is the source of an absolute and
unwavering belief I have in the best of you.

I have had many different glimpses of a Higher Power,

which have been enough for me to believe in something far
bigger than myself at work in my life. Here are a few of them:

I knew the HP gave you to me against all odds when I first
felt you flutter inside my belly, when you would say "Not the
mama" to every person who wasn't me. I smiled and knew
there had to be something in the world bigger and greater than
me to be blessed with the gift of you.

When you cut your finger, when you were lost in Key West,
when the jellyfish attacked you, when you tried to "kill" your
little brother, when you almost drowned in the Wilsons' pool,
when you started smoking, I knew the guardian angel stepped
in, put things back together, and kept us safe. I could hear it:
It isn't his time. He should be saved because he will do good
in the world. That is another glimpse at a Higher Power—you
have lived when you might have perished.

I felt the Higher Power as a whisper in my ear that our
home was no longer a safe and nurturing place for you, which
helped me summon the courage to leave Sioux City and move
to Omaha. I felt confident that we could make it on our own
and start a new life together.

A Higher Power was working in my life when I remembered
Jackson, the place where I worked twenty-five years ago with
kids just like you. I had an office there on the sixth floor, in
the very building you are staying in. I helped prepare all those
years ago for your arrival. It was an HP that gave me strength
to leave you there, and I believe it was your HP that helped
open up your heart and mind to help you see that you should
stay and do this hard thing. When you feel unsure and in
doubt, just know your HP is strong and at work on your behalf.

I describe my Higher Power as grace, mercy, forgiveness, redemption, and comeback. The truth that sets you free instead of doing you in. A Higher Power is whatever brings you hope. When you see hawks and eagles, when you know that people are on your side, when you know that Grandma and Grandpa and Tim are cheering for you, when you realize that your mama loves you unconditionally, when you see miracles like redemption and people willing to forgive you and each other, when you see that what you resent and think you can't forgive never really happened, when you feel in your gut that you are totally loved, that is Higher Power. You get a glimpse of your true, amazing, loved self in the reflection of a Higher Power.

Your mama can love you unconditionally because I see the Higher Power at work in you, a perfect reflection of God. I will hold you in my arms for a while and in my heart forever because I know that you are good and kind and amazing and perfect. I know that you are a manifestation of God. I see it in you every day—even when you cannot.

Sweetie, it is because of you, and all the miracles going on in your life right now, that I know for sure that a Higher Power exists. I see the proof in those moments when we can no longer help ourselves, and a powerful force picks us up and takes us to a place where we will find grace. You are in a place your mother helped create long before you were born, a place she was called to but didn't know why. It was a call she could not refuse. She trusted that her work would be for good and couldn't know it would be a place that would help save her son. An HP gives us the bravery to say yes when put in a seemingly impossible place. It enables the courage to stay, to forgive, to dream about living differently.

It is the Higher Power that brings us together in the knowledge that we are all scared, we all want to be loved. We want to wake up and understand our world. The minute we can see our scared self in another, and realize we can offer relief and unconditional love, we are God on earth. We see the Higher Power when we look past others' behavior to see the scared, lonely child, when we feel connection and are able to give mercy, to find forgiveness. We summon the energy for hope and second chances.

My prayer to my Higher Power is often a simple "Thank you." I pray this to my God, to my people in heaven, and to my friends on earth who are connected to me at a soul level. They gather together to give me what I need, even when I have no idea that I need.

There is a moment of hope when a monumental shift takes place—an awakening. Suddenly, we see things in a radical new way, and the tears of relief fall because the courage of two people did not go unrewarded. The sight of miracles can be almost blinding, and they are definitely humbling as we are reminded that the simple act of surrendering—that simple first step—lets us fall away from ego, pain, deceit, and separation. We find the arms of the kind and wonderful God we cannot yet name or can't yet admit is real. We are so tired and so scared and then so grateful that we landed in a soft place so we could heal. We realize that we were never really lost, and could never fall too far, because we were never in charge.

Son, I wish for you mercy and fresh starts. I give you

unconditional love and forgiveness and recognition of the
perfection of who you are right now. In my presence, you
need *never* feel like you are not enough. I will be your "in the
meantime plan" until you realize that when we are at our best,
highest self, we are a Higher Power manifested here on earth.
So if you can't believe in the big, believe in the shadow. I will
do my best to witness you and to be the best mortal example of
what it feels like to be in the presence of a Higher Power.

A Higher Power lives in each of us, son. It is your best self,
your kindest heart, your most hopeful, seeking mind, your
most audacious dream, and your peace at night when you come
to know you are perfect even when you feel flawed. My favorite
song, which Grandma Mary sang to you the day you were born,
is "Amazing Grace." Amazing grace will come to you. It will find
you, I promise.

The incredible power of God is that for a long while, others
can believe on your behalf. You simply need to believe in those
who love you unconditionally. Surround yourself with amazing
people who are on the same path. Let their insight help you
find your insight, their breakthrough your breakthrough, their
freedom your freedom. One day, if you believe in those people
who believe in you, God will be revealed. You will come to
know that you are God, a perfect replica, and you'll feel it in
your belly and your soul. All will be good because all about you
is good.

If I could love you up, teach you what I know to be true,
and save you from the hard lessons at hand, I would. I wish I
could leverage my own painful lessons to save you trouble and
pain. But I cannot keep you from your path or regret it. A great

teacher of mine once asked me, "If you knew that this was your son's only path to God, would you take it from him?" The answer is a resounding "NO!" I am so grateful for my path, and for you and for your path.

Honey, YOU are my proof that God exists! You are evidence that mercy is abundant, that miracles happen. You are an old soul, and you know so much. I know heavy things are swirling in your head, things that have always been a mystery to you. The veil between the worlds is thin for you. Knowing is a big responsibility. I know from my own experience how tempting it is to seek an escape. Now is your time to stop seeking escapes and to answer the call to leadership so that you can heal yourself and help others.

Please know that you are loved, you are my beloved, you are my miracle, and you are blessed. Open your heart. Open your mind. That is enough—what you need will be delivered and bestowed upon you. I promise and cross my heart.

Love you,
Mama Cy

LOVE BIG AND LET GO

The sacred space that stretches between loving big and letting go is called heartbreak. You can't escape it. You shouldn't try.

Almost always, an aching of the heart is the natural outcome of loving another. The ache begins the minute we are asked—or are required—to let go but cannot yet find a way to loosen our grip on what we so desired and needed and enjoyed.

A natural tendency is to see heartbreak as a failure, a sign that something ended that shouldn't have, an implication that we could have, should have, done more to contribute to a continuing. We see heartbreak as something to avoid and to protect ourselves from. Thinking like this ignores the inevitable ending of all things.

Looked at another way, life with no heartbreak would signal muted, narrow living. In my view, heartbreak can also be seen as an accolade, a congratulatory message of love that was big, hope that was pure, and effort that was sincere. Traversing the space between love and loss in life is inevitable, and if you can open your mind and soul to the journey, you will emerge a little more evolved each time.

Although heartbreak comes in many shapes and iterations, among the most powerful ways to experience its evolutionary powers is to develop a warm, comfortable relationship with death, which is the paramount loss, the ultimate heartbreak.

I was lucky enough to welcome death as my "professor for life" at a fairly young age. One experience in particular helped me stop seeing it through the narrow lens of loss and understand that it required a broader spectrum of emotions.

As a young social worker, I was asked to check on the well-being of a father, an immigrant from Africa, whose six-year-old daughter had been killed in a bicycle accident. Medical workers who saw him at the hospital were worried because he wasn't showing what they considered the "appropriate emotion" of a grieving father. He wasn't hysterical. He didn't sob uncontrollably. They thought he might be in shock.

I went out to his home a few days later to check on him and, without making assumptions, asked how he was doing. Hospital workers were a little concerned, I told him, that he hadn't seemed sad.

In his tradition, wallowing in sadness would have made him a selfish, substandard parent. His daughter had a short, blessed life. When he thought of her, he told me, he could only feel grateful and happy. "She tasted the very sweetest part of life," he said. She'd had six years of being cherished by everyone around her. Six years of never knowing heartbreak or rejection or loss. The chubby little legs that had pedaled the bike had only known cuddles and kisses, never the ridicule of junior high peers. She hadn't discovered, and never would, that the world can sometimes be unkind.

"How can I be sad about a child who lived the most perfect part of life?" he asked. "How can I not smile when I think about her and her good fortune?" She was gone, but she had not "lost" her life. She had lived all six years of it fully, in great love, until she died. The pain of loss was for those left behind, which mostly sprang from thoughts of the future. He felt sad if he thought of all the things they might have done together and never would, which meant his suffering was tied to a never-promised future. But his daughter? Well, she had lived the best part anyone gets. Over that, he could not suffer.

I percolated on his view of death for a long time. It wasn't that this father felt no grief or heartbreak, but like all parents, he wanted the best for his child. And in his mind, she'd experienced the best, most pure part of life. If the price of loving her was heartbreak, he was willing, even happy, to pay it. But he refused to let the grief obscure his vision of the beautiful.

Death and loss are inevitable. It makes sense that grief and sadness will assert themselves as natural, appropriate emotions. However, if they are the only emotions you allow to reside in your heart and body during heartbreak, you're in danger of seriously missing the point of a fully experienced life.

Everyone you love will eventually leave you, or you will leave them. We know this to be a fact, and yet we allow ourselves to be completely shocked and knocked off center when it happens. It almost seems silly, doesn't it?

I'm not saying "Yay, death." Not at all. I am just saying death happens. If we allow it, death can be a superlative instructor in the art of letting go and a profoundly powerful force in our own evolution.

I was with my grandparents, my mom, my dad, my sister-in-law, brother-in-law, and my best friend Cathy in the last years, months, and the final day of their lives. With them, I got the long good-bye. I've also experienced the sudden death of a brother and a nephew. I've learned not to back away from death. I tend to walk toward it when others retreat. In fact, I often find myself in the front-row seat. Perhaps because I have learned to be fully present to dying, others seem to welcome my company in the final stage of living.

I believe that if I don't allow everyone and everything to be my teacher, then I am a terrible student. And my times with the dying and the grieving have shaped how I live in extraordinary ways. Amidst the shards of great heartbreak over death, I've been able to recognize the big love I've been blessed to give and receive and marry that love with gratitude and joy. So many names have been written indelibly on my heart that it's become a cracked, graffiti-covered wall.

Heartbreak, if you put out a welcome mat when it arrives, can help you become exquisitely good at letting go. By looking at death not as the end but rather as a developmental stage in life, both become a practice, something to get skilled at. Your broken heart will thrust you into a spacious, rich, more profound life.

THE "GOOD" DEATH

I'm not saying I have this death thing figured out yet, but I always welcome its lessons. I got several of them while working for hospice, and one in particular stands out.

One day my coworker Ruth, soon to become a dear friend, called to ask if I would like to "attend a death." I hadn't worked in hospice long. Mostly I had shadowed people—nurses, caregivers, the chaplain—as they tended to the actively dying.

The words Ruth used got my attention. When she picked me up, I asked why she used the phrase "attend a death." She explained to me we would be there mostly as witnesses, to provide support and caring. We weren't participants.

This woman, dying of cancer, was someone I'd met before. She hadn't been the easiest hospice client. She often drank until she was incoherent or unconscious. She would insist that her caregivers get her out of bed and wheel her outside so she could smoke cigarettes. She was often cantankerous.

When we arrived at her house, the atmosphere was tense. Several people had arrived to say good-bye, and in some cases, the woman refused to see them. There were arguments and anger and acrimony—not the scene I was expecting as a death attendant. Ruth and I were there until the literal bitter end.

On the way home, Ruth asked how I was doing. "What a horrible death!" I blurted, a little shocked by what I had witnessed.

"Oh, that was a good death," Ruth replied gently. The woman had received support, comfort, and the medications she needed to keep her out of pain.

I didn't judge it that way. To me, her death wasn't even in the vicinity of being loving or peaceful. I went through the litany of things I'd witnessed that, in my mind, qualified as a bad ending. "How can you tell me that was a good death?" I asked.

"Oh, Cy, I have good news," she said. "That was *her* death. And you know what? The even better news is that you get your own death. When it's your turn to die, hopefully you'll get to do it however you want."

I quickly understood the simplest part of her words, that how the client chose to exit this life wasn't for me to judge. But it took me a while to fully understand what she meant, and I thought about it a lot. Of course, we want to prolong life for ourselves and those we love, but when death can be clearly seen in the distance, beauty also beckons for those willing to go all in to find it. I don't know if there is such a thing as a "perfect death," but if you've lived with connection and meaning and purpose, it's likely to get you closer.

My initial time with hospice definitely set me on a path of making peace with my own mortality. Knowing my time was limited made me feel pressured to figure out how to live my life well to increase the odds of a "good death." The question seemed so big, and the answers complicated and elusive. Then I found a quote from Ram Dass that spoke to me with its simplicity and raw truth:

> If I'm going to die, the best way to prepare is to quiet
>   my mind and open my heart.
> If I'm going to live, the best way to prepare is to quiet
>   my mind and open my heart.

Working at hospice, helping people who are taking leave of their bodies, taught me there is worthy work to be done no matter how short your time on earth might be. The facilitation of this last stage of life isn't only about relieving pain and providing comfort. It promises the ultimate opportunity for personal growth. The last stage of life can be a full-blown stage in development—just like childhood, adolescence, and adulthood. Dying needn't be merely enduring until the end or frantically fighting to evade it. Big work can be done in sense-making, integrating, and concluding. It's a time for reflection about the questions of meaningful life and what comes next. It's when you get to give your final gifts, like forgiveness, wisdom, perspective, and expressions of love.

If you're willing to closely accompany those dying, you will be transformed for the better if you allow it. To make death only about loss and trauma is so short-sighted. Why not include transformation, restoration, and celebration? Grief and loss and pity can be like quicksand dragging you inexorably down into the muck, or you can look up and around to see the beauty in the interactions and experiences of those who are leaving and those who will remain for now.

My best friend Cathy died as I was writing this book, surrounded by her family and me. Walking along closely with friend Cathy Frost as she was dying, and as she died, changed me in ways I am still discovering.

I remember so clearly the wise advice a woman gave me soon after I'd moved to a new town. I was young, I knew no one, and I was struggling. "Find your people," she said. But who are they, I asked? How will I know them? "Just ask their name, and then check your heart," she said. "Their name will be written there. It will feel like a reunion with someone you've been looking for."

When I found Cathy, at a routine marketing meeting at work, she was clad in trademark polka dots and was quite wary of me. Still, I somehow knew her name was inscribed on my heart. "We're going to become the best of friends," I assured her, but my prediction proved too modest. Over our thirty-plus-year relationship, we became soulmates in the truest sense of the word.

After being diagnosed with late-stage cancer, she managed the remaining three and a half years of her life doing an elegant dance. She was determined to die the same way she lived, by getting everything she could from what living while dying offers. Cathy made conscious choices to wring every drop of learning from the experience. She sought knowledge, never stopped asking questions, and concluded unfinished business with compassion. She continued teaching me by describing what it was like to die. She loved big. She did as much to have a good death as anyone can.

Her one remaining fear was not about death, she confided to me one day. It was that she might be forgotten. I had recently traveled to Egypt, so I could describe to her what people there believe. People die twice, I told her, first when they leave their body and second when their name is spoken for the last time. I assured her I intend to keep speaking her name. I made a promise I am confident I can keep. Since her name is truly written on my heart, I would speak her name not just in my stories of us but each time I helped another person. That helped ease Cathy's heartbreak of leaving me.

Knowing Cathy changed me for the better. The version of me that meets the world today is full of Cathy. My belief is that when you've allowed another to fully enter your heart, they are as much a part of you as your DNA is and can't ever be lost. That helps ease my own heartbreak.

THE THINNEST VEIL

Each time I have had the privilege to be with someone moving from life to death, I've witnessed their ability to understand that life is finite and yet connected to something much larger than their physical body. They believed that a part of them would go on.

A sweet magic infuses those moments, amplifying feelings in a way that can dramatically transform and change your approach to living. The presence of death supercharges minds and hearts, heightening the experience of love and connection. At least, it has been that way for me. I am determined to Love Big, so learning to let go has been among life's great and necessary gifts.

The veil between the worlds becomes thin when someone is preparing to leave this one. It is such a sacred time. In my experience, it's an amazing resolution of all contradictions, a moment in time when there is room for all of it. The certainty of being part of something ineffable, recognizing the being that is unable to be contained or harmed or ended, is beautifully entwined with a sense of vulnerability, being small and extinguishable. The confidence of being part of an undefeatable greatness peacefully coexists with the helplessness of realizing we are but a tiny moment in time. Being witness to that gives you a glimpse into everything making sense while knowing at the same time that you don't need to understand *anything* to live with meaning. It's a whiff of the glory that we have at our disposal every moment of our lives.

People are grateful to someone who is willing to be fully present in the space of dying. Until you experience that, there is a kind of empathy you cannot embody. It is a privilege to witness.

And death also has much to teach us even when it is abrupt and unexpected.

SNOW ANGELS

Tap, tap, tap.

It was early in the morning, way too early for someone to be tapping on my window, damn it.

A few months after my mom died, I had driven to my hometown to help my family go through her things as we settled the estate. I'd arrived late at night, as a snowstorm blew in, and I was exhausted. Tap, tap, tap. I groaned and rolled over.

My brother Tim had arisen early to shovel the driveways of some of the older people in town. It was 6 a.m. His tapping was an invitation to come out and play like we'd done as kids, when he wanted a co-conspirator without our dad finding out what we were up to.

"The snow is amazing!" he mouthed. "Come out!" I waved him away and tried to get back to sleep. Blessed silence for a while, and then tap, tap, tap.

He'd returned to the window, this time holding up a box of donuts from Casey's, the best in town. Whoa, that was upping the ante. I wavered but shook my head. "Come ON!" he hollered, falling backward to make a snow angel.

I was laughing as I threw on a coat and pulled boots over my pajamas. Tim and I went from yard to yard, making a snow angel in every fresh snowbank we encountered. We were kids again, hooting with laughter.

After our fun, we straggled into the local diner for breakfast, me with crazy bedhead and still in my pajamas. As people we knew came over to greet us, they gave me strange looks. Tim shook his head sadly: "Yeah, she's not doing so well, but I'm working with her." And we cracked up anew.

The next day, Tim was dead. His heart gave out from a condition sometimes called "the widow maker." We had been so close. He was snatched away so quickly.

His sudden disappearance from the world (though never my heart) delivered another huge lesson that rings often in my ears, usually in Tim's voice: The snow is fresh only for a while. The sweet, ordinary experience we shared, coupled with death, dramatically transformed my approach to life.

I've been a person to hold back, to follow the rules. I see "Do Not Disturb" signs where they don't exist. I've not always allowed myself to jump into the spontaneity of the moment. But after Tim's death, the experience of making snow angels with my baby brother was supercharged, surging the lesson into my heart and the marrow of my bones. To this day, when I hesitate over doing something that makes me feel vulnerable, when I hang back from jumping into something silly but pleasurable, I hear his voice. "What else do you have to do right now? Why not go for it?" I've learned not to miss the magical moments that come with spontaneity.

I couldn't have prepared for Tim's sudden death, but I did one thing exactly right. I answered the tap on the window.

LOVE AND LOSS

One lesson about death has been consistently underscored: The loss is not the other's.

In my experience, people tend to make their peace with leaving this dream we call life, solid in a supreme knowing they never were separate from a loving source and that their return to that is welcoming, not frightening. All loss—a death, a divorce, a job—belongs to you, the one remaining. It is up to you to do the work of grieving and letting go.

Perhaps my sweet philosopher boy said it best. When I told my young son Will that his grandmother was dying, his response showed a wisdom that belied his short life experience:

"That's sad," Will said. "I wasn't done knowing her yet."

And isn't that the essence of heartbreak? We just weren't done knowing them. Our suffering comes from wanting them back so our lives are more comfortable. Life with my mom alive felt safer and softer. She was the one I turned to in tough situations. She was generous with her wisdom and forgiveness. She loved big, she was always there for me, and I wanted her by my side longer. So the loss of her was mine. And the heartbreak was real. It was a hard letting go, because we just weren't done knowing her yet.

Maybe that's why it is such a struggle to let go. We fear loss. We fear the pain. We fear that limbo of living the life in between what was before but won't be again and the one we create next. Maybe our biggest fear of losing someone is that it will reveal what we have failed to notice and the things we never got around to repairing. Panic arises knowing that there are things not yet risked, not yet accomplished. Maybe we thought we had more time to express remorse, to forgive, and to be forgiven.

It has been said that if you can overcome the fear of death, you will lose all other fears in life.

Not surprisingly, our old friend ego is at the heart of this natural, fundamental fear. It is tied up in identity, the physical body, the externality of life. As Eckhart Tolle wrote, "Only the ego dies." No wonder it wants to keep us trapped in a fear of death, which makes us run even when there is clearly nowhere to go. I've often wondered how many people's fear of death is tied to their fear over how they live.

I've had two near-death experiences. One I don't remember, because I was a toddler when it happened. The other experience I remember vividly because the way I felt as it happened was so surprising. While vacationing in Mexico, I foolishly went swimming in the wild waters that everyone warns you to avoid. The waves were voracious. I was knocked down and tumbled around like a pile of clothes in a washing machine, my head banging against the ocean floor. I remember thinking clearly, "The next breath I take will be water, and I will die." I felt remarkably calm about it. "How weird that it would end like this," I thought.

The next thing I remember was violently coughing up sea water, surrounded by my panicked husband and friends. I was alive. And my fear of death was dead.

I'd be foolish to predict how my actual death will play out. Perhaps my survival instinct will reign supreme, and fear will assert itself after all. But I do know I want to wring every possible lesson out of whatever happens while I'm living.

The easiest way to let go is to stop hanging on. Stop being private with your love, stop being stingy with your forgiveness, stop clinging to your resentments. Release your righteousness. Someone once told me that if you want to love big and live big, eleven simple words, used daily, will become the work of your whole life: I love you. Please forgive me. I forgive you. Thank you.

If you haven't taken the opportunity to use these words on the daily, you can seize the opening presented near the end of life. Using those words in the space just before death, with authentic expression from the heart, will conspire with you to find resolution and peace.

And if you can't make that happen, honor the one who died by living differently, by repeating that kind of prayer in your heart and out loud to others you care about.

PRACTICING DEATH

Learning to let go becomes easier if you practice death. I like practice sessions and dry runs, especially for the things I worry about doing well—like death. I figure practicing death will help me craft a good conclusion to the story.

You have opportunities to practice the skills of dying and letting go every day—and not just from experiencing the death of others. Heartbreak can be found in many places. Because I have chosen, again and again, to love big and live big, I am often driven to my knees by the heartbreak of loss and the process of letting go. I've made big mistakes along the way.

Practice is the real-life stuff where you might be tempted to cheat the lesson. You might be tempted to dull or eliminate heartbreak by telling yourself "I didn't care that much" or "That person didn't deserve me." You save your tears for the hidden, late-night hours. You try rewriting the story, to lessen the sting of loss, so it includes only the horrible parts. Maybe you jump into new relationships too quickly. I have tried to push down the aching by diving into my work and narrowing my world. I withdraw from others with justification that the fewer connections I have, the less I can be hurt.

If someone has died, the world will manufacture stories and offer them up to you as a way of avoiding heartbreak. People will talk about why it was for the best, how someone is no longer suffering. They attempt to give full permission to spiritually bypass the pain by saying they're "in a better place."

That never works for me. The only path to truly letting go is by leaning in to the hurt. In fact, heartbreak seems to be a painful, powerful, and necessary contraction to birth whatever is next in life.

Each heartbreak is a kind of death and delivers me to a deeper level, a re-remembering of an old truth, a maturation of my spiritual progress. Without heartbreaks, I suspect that I would have remained longer in the shallows, falsely believing that my happiness is related to my circumstances or good fortune. Eventually, I fully inhabit that space between the life I loved and a new life that I will eventually love. That's where I find growth and evolution.

I recommend practicing the fine art of letting go daily through "mini deaths" of the ego. This can be as simple as questioning your thoughts, examining your stories, or fully embracing humiliating experiences that leave the ego bruised and gasping for air.

Meditation is another form of practicing death I am dedicated to. It unhooks me from the external for a commune with the internal, where I often find connection to the peaceful and blissful divine.

And I even practice the physical act of dying at least a couple of times a week. At the end of a yoga practice, the teacher calls for savasana, also known as corpse pose. This pose is done lying down, eyes closed, body completely relaxed. You withdraw the senses, integrating what you have done and learned. The rigors of the physical practice are over. You rest in peace by sinking deeper into your mat and fully surrendering to the exhaustion of a challenging practice.

I look forward to savasana every single time. I actually crave it. I think about it on the drive to class—anticipating the time when we finally get to do savasana.

Finding connection with this metaphor brings me comfort when I think about my loved ones who have died. Thoughts of savasana helped me ease the heartache after my sweet fourteen-year-old nephew Drew unexpectedly died in a car accident. I thought about being in the middle of a complicated, strenuous pose and having my teacher call out, "Time for savasana!" If that happened, I wouldn't even be mad. I'd be absolutely thrilled. I'd think that was an amazing, compassionate teacher to bring me such blissful surrender and peaceful rest earlier in the session.

I don't fear death today. I think about death as the best savasana ever.

In the meantime, I will keep practicing the art of letting go and willingly accept the inevitable next heartbreak as proof that I dared to love big once again.

TIM'S NEW SUIT

My beloved mother died in 2005. As our family planned her funeral services, we each had a role. My brothers would be the pallbearers. My younger brother, Tim, worried about how he'd look.

In my family, going to church meant putting on your very best clothing, dressing up as a way of honoring God. For my mother's service, the standard felt even higher because we'd be honoring her, too. Tim believed showing up in his regular clothes would be an affront. He fretted he wouldn't look as good as our brothers did as they carried her coffin. We'd always been close, and I knew he didn't have a lot of money. He asked me for a special favor: Could I help him out, buy him a suit? Yes, of course. It truly would be my honor.

"I'm going to look amazing," he said, his eyes bright with excitement. He went to the department store and, as he told us later, felt completely lost. He was not trained in the art of shopping and wandered around, trying to figure it out. Finally, a sales clerk approached and asked if she could help. "Yeah," he said, "I need a suit for my mother's funeral. I'm going to be a pall-bearer. I really need to look like a million bucks." He didn't know where to start. But she did.

The clerk took him completely under her wing. She identified suits she thought he'd look great in, then tracked down perfect, crisp dress shirts to go with them, and matching ties. She assured him they could get everything tailored to a perfect fit. For nearly two hours, she scouted, and he tried on clothes, cracked jokes, and laughed. Tim told us they had a blast.

The clerk saw a man who wanted to honor his mother by looking great, and she wanted to help. He left the store feeling fulfilled and excited. She did something that likely wasn't in her job description: she made Tim feel like a million bucks.

After Mom's service, as we gathered for the reception, Tim made sure that people checked out his stylish attire. He would grab random people by the elbow, cracking, "Don't I look great? Seriously, have you ever seen me look this amazing?" He'd strike a pose and demand I take a photo. "You gotta capture this. I might never look this good again!"

Less than four months later, at the age of thirty-six, my sweet brother Tim died unexpectedly from heart failure. The clerk who'd helped him at the store recognized his photo from the obituary. She called to tell us she remembered Tim well. They'd had such a great time, she told us, and she had felt so much satisfaction in helping Tim find the perfect suit.

What she couldn't have known is that her small act of generosity ended up having enormous meaning to our family. Our final view of Tim was in his casket, dressed in the suit she had so carefully helped him choose.

He looked like a million bucks.

CHOSEN

If you don't live in the world of choosing, you live in the world of excusing.

—James Altucher

In the roiling wake of my first divorce, my sons asked me why I had married their dad.

My first impulse was to list the qualities that attracted me to him: he was good-looking, a college graduate, a professional, we had things in common, we both wanted a family. But in the end, I blurted out the real reason, which shocked even me in its authenticity:

I married him because he asked me.

We revisited the question as my second marriage was foundering. Why did you marry him? my sons asked. And I was disheartened to realize that, if I were completely transparent, the answer was the same, with one little nuance. I married my second husband because he *finally* asked.

Two huge life decisions with considerable consequences were made on a wave of exhilaration over being chosen.

This revelation was startling because, in both instances, I had failed to do a thorough check-in with the person who should have mattered the most—me. The thrill of finally being chosen by men I saw as desirable obscured the questions I should have been asking: Were we right for each other? Did I want them as life companions? Did I really desire the life we might have together? Could we withstand the relationship rigors required of a long marriage?

I was so excited that they asked me to marry them that I failed to ask myself if I *wanted* to marry them. If it was a *good idea* to marry them. Some life lessons I've learned in the hardest, most painful way.

CRAVING TO BE CHOSEN

Yearning to belong, to be wanted, and to feel included is a natural human instinct. We all experience the tension of wanting to be chosen for kickball, to be asked to the dance, to get the promotion. It's not necessarily an emotional dysfunction. The instinct that makes us want to belong can help us behave in ways that facilitate connection and community. For a group considering whether to include you, behavior that demonstrates wanting to belong can reduce the risk associated with including you. Wanting to be seen and recognized for your qualities and contributions is normal.

However, when the line between needing to be chosen and honoring self gets so blurred that it's practically invisible, it's time to step back and look more closely at what is really going on. If being the *chosen one* is paramount, it's easier to abandon your values or standards for someone you may love but who isn't the best choice for you. If you were looking clearly at the relationship through the lens of your needs, desires, and best interests, you might not consciously or intentionally choose this person for yourself. When the decision is based on the excitement of being chosen, you'll likely eventually lose yourself in the contortions of doing whatever is required to continue being chosen.

Healthy relationships require a balance of independence and mutuality. When it came to my two primary romantic relationships, the validation of "being chosen" was such a prevailing force that I took myself out of the equation. My ability to counterbalance the cost of being chosen with self-advocacy was underdeveloped. Saying a loving "no, thank you" in relationships that had potential to strain my emotional budget required a level of self-assurance that I apparently lacked.

In my first marriage, I could blame youth, naivete, and insecurity for my eagerness to be chosen. The second time, I saw myself as wiser, stronger, financially successful, and confident, yet that didn't forestall me from ignoring the relationship's early red flags. I sailed right through several stop signs. Being chosen preempted a clear view of reality and self-awareness.

Having left my first marriage with enormous financial debt, a bargain I struck to retain custody of my sons, I had the sense to suggest a prenuptial agreement before marrying a second time. It wasn't necessary, my intended argued, because my business was a "premarital asset," and therefore it would be protected, mine alone. He was so convincing in his arguments that I squelched my impulse to insist we discuss it with a legal expert. I worried if I did, it would threaten his choosing me and ruin the fairy tale I believed we were coauthoring. It never occurred to me he would subtly twist the meanings of his words to slowly lay claim to assets I'd established from twenty-five years of creation.

I didn't dare risk my "chosen" status by insisting on a thorough discussion of something I had strong feelings about. And that was just one example of the myriad times I caved in throughout our relationship, each instance adding a hash mark to the emotional cost of belonging. Eventually, I was carrying an emotional debt with an unreasonable, outrageous interest rate. It was unsustainable. Emotional bankruptcy felt inevitable unless I made drastic decisions.

In the financial sense, my experience was a familiar reenactment of the extortion my brothers used to demand on money I had earned on my own. After our marriage, my husband asserted a coauthorship and an ownership of the business I had created as he criticized how I managed my finances and my business. He also wasn't shy about giving me feedback about my deficits as a parent and a person.

I had a starring role to play in that dynamic. We had these kinds of arguments even before we got married, but I forged ahead because, after all, he'd chosen me.

LOSING THE KRYPTONITE CRAVINGS

The second marriage dissolution was much more disheartening than the first. How had I, once again, outsourced my validation as a worthy woman who is confident about my desirability and the great value that I contribute to a relationship?

The ego has a special talent for creating the yearning to be chosen at all costs. As I set about cleaning up the mess of my second marriage, I realized if I were ever to establish a balanced, emotional relationship with a man, I needed to understand these kryptonite cravings. I had to evolve to the point where I could choose myself first. Self-love, a clear-eyed view of reality, and internal validation needed to be at the center of my choices if I were going to successfully set aside the need for external validation in my love relationships.

As usual, it meant excavating old wounds. My high school and college days could be characterized as a dating desert—I rarely got asked out. The one serious relationship I had in college did not end well. He was handsome, athletic, popular, and charming. I was so wild about him that I set aside my own values to keep up with his partying ways. It became pretty obvious that we weren't going to work out after I walked in on him having sex with my good friend. The implosion of that abusive relationship sent me into such a black emotional downward spiral that it took months of deep personal work to recover.

As a young woman, I found myself swirling in whirlpools of resentment as I watched everyone else seemingly easily obtain what I thought I wanted. Oh, to be a wife! To snag someone who would love me exclusively, a handsome and gallant protector. I wanted a partner, a man who would help me create a family, traditions, a future. I yearned for the benefits of the fairy tale, a safe corner in the world with a man who consistently demonstrated to the world that I was, and would always be, his chosen one.

When my first husband asked me to marry him, it was a dream come true. Someone had chosen me! His proposal was so flattering, so validating of my worthiness as a woman, that the only possible answer was an enthusiastic, emphatic "yes." He had asked, so of course it was decided.

For twenty years, we created what I thought was a decent marriage, raising four sons and building a life. I justified the compromises, self-sacrifice, and challenges as the price of being chosen. It's what I did to be a great partner and to keep my status as the chosen one. And I willingly, happily wrote those emotional checks until the day I discovered I had actually been chosen so he could avoid hard truths in his own life that he was unwilling to reconcile. Suddenly the safe place I thought we had created felt decidedly dangerous. Among other things, my exclusivity as the object of his desire was an illusion. My marriage, my world, my life, came crashing down. My ego spent time in intensive care, completely shattered and barely hanging on.

But eventually my ego recovered enough to persuade me that next time, NEXT TIME, I would be so much wiser. I would spot the red flags long before they unfurled. A lesson had been learned. I would be the choosy one!

And then I met future husband No. 2. Notice the theme here: He was funny, smart, charming, and good-looking. My ego spun new stories about how he could be a perfect partner, the real deal, the one who could help me restore the family life I felt robbed of.

We found each other online, and I was flattered when he began texting me, calling me. Soon after we met, love-infused dopamine was inundating my senses. When I got wind that he was also texting and calling other women, I batted away my doubts. We hadn't made commitments to each other, so no harm, no foul.

Even after we decided to date exclusively, he dangled the possibility of choosing me like a glass slipper found at the ball. We were so in love, but he wouldn't tell his friends or ex-wife about me until he was *sure*. I couldn't meet his kids until he trusted I was "*the one.*" I doubled down on my efforts to be the chosen one. I performed for his love and waited for him to share my vision of a storybook future. We would join our families, become the Brady Bunch with a bigger dose of testosterone. After he was fired from his senior-level job, I brought him into my company. We would work together and create a more vivid, more beautiful, more perfect life.

And while we both were enthused about those possibilities, still he withheld a marriage proposal. He set up situations where I was sure he was about to propose, until he didn't. When I got grumpy about it, he would tease me, saying he had something far grander and more magical in mind.

As it turned out, he did. He dropped down on his knee at the Taj Mahal on Valentine's Day (in the U.S., if not India), on a combination business/pleasure trip (paid for by me). Two weeks before, I'd been in tears over how he'd refused to stand up for me with his ex-wife. I had noted "his capacity for nastiness" in my journal. And the night before he proposed, we'd had a huge fight. It didn't matter. He'd finally chosen me! My rose-colored glasses obscured the bright red flags that had been waving for weeks.

We began planning a beautiful lakeside wedding. I traveled

to New York City to purchase my wedding dress, the fulfillment of a dream, and was asked to be on an episode of TLC's *Say Yes to the Dress*. All the while, I paid the bills while my fiancé complained about the budget.

And thus began our marriage, in which my pattern of acquiescence and lack of boundaries showed up present and accounted for. Subconsciously, I continued to fear he would stop choosing me. I complied, conformed, and compromised. I was willing to advocate for myself but had agreed to a relationship that required constant advocacy in order not to feel taken advantage of. My ego's stories obscured the fact that my need to be chosen outweighed the necessity of being true to myself. And when it all fell apart again, over financial resources, parenting styles, and equitability, I sat amidst the rubble completely perplexed at how such a strong, smart, successful woman could have made the same ill-considered choice twice.

Why the hell did I keep choosing to measure my worth based on someone else's flawed appraisals?

DIVORCE AS AN ACT OF INTEGRITY

The last thing I wanted was for this second marriage to fall apart, so I worked overtime trying to find solutions that I could live with, that would make him keep choosing me, that would keep us in relationship. I worked an even crazier schedule because he demanded a 50 percent share of everything I earned, which he defined as "marital assets."

When the frictions of our blended family of eight boys threatened to consume our relationship, I paid for another house nearby to mitigate our wildly disparate parenting styles. It seemed like the most elegant, if expensive, solution to keeping the peace. I endured long negotiations about how much money I should turn over in the name of "our" business, which was based on my intellectual property and the goodwill I had generated with clients long before I met him. The work I did required a grueling schedule of travel, for weeks at a time, while he stayed home and fashioned a lifestyle that allowed him to take flying instruction and attend his kids' sporting events and music lessons. I tried for four years, without success, to negotiate a kind of postnuptial agreement that would allow me to keep what had been mine before we married. He refused to sign papers that would ensure my sons' inheritance. More flashbacks to my childhood, a time when I constantly negotiated with siblings who demanded I turn over to them what I alone had earned.

I kept up the work because I truly loved him and because staying felt like integrity. We had made commitments. Like the title of our wedding song, "I Won't Give Up on Us," I felt really, really strongly that I should finish the marathon, even though I was out of breath, exhausted, and in pain. I continued to create assets and turn over half, while he created very few and turned over none. Did it feel balanced or just? Never. But still, giving up didn't seem like an option.

Then one day, in a stark moment of clarity, I realized that not giving up on us meant I had totally given up on me. I thought about all the times I had been treated unfairly. The many instances where I had been hurt that others hadn't stood up for me. But why should anyone go to bat for me when I was so reluctant to do the same? How could I realistically expect others to do what I wouldn't do for myself?

My perspective shifted. For years, I willingly abandoned my need for equity, for fairness, for mutual respect, for peace. It was time to take a stand for me, to choose me. I needed to know that I was loved for who I am. Period. I wanted and deserved equitable, mutually beneficial relationships. Those who were on board with that would remain in my orbit. Others might decide to go, and I'd have to learn acceptance and serenity if they made that choice.

My self-advocacy had crept up to a bright line that I hadn't dared cross because the risk of losing my chosen status felt too monumental. It could initiate a great abandonment by someone I truly loved. Even so, I knew my integrity needed to be centered on my commitment to me. For relationships to flourish, for this marriage to survive, I needed to know that l was loved for who I was, not for what I could provide. Staying felt like self-betrayal in the guise of integrity. It was time to stop keeping the external peace while I waged an internal war. It was time to fight for me.

In the realization of that surrender came the recognition that I had once again managed to create the familiar. While my husband saw our problematic issue as money, for me it was about equity and fairness, something I had often been denied in my big, everyone-for-themselves family. I needed to settle a childhood score to settle my soul. The resemblance between my marriage and my family of origin was too strong to ignore. But I was no longer a child. I was an adult. No longer would I be willing to buy another's love. I was determined to heal my wound by standing before him as a woman who knew her worth, not as a child performing for his love.

After exhausting myself with years of sharing, problem-solving, asking, proposing, pleading, and spreadsheeting, I asked him for a do-over—a resetting of the non-negotiables in our marriage. I hadn't stopped loving him, but I had found new love for myself.

I proposed a financial divorce, but I really wanted to stay together and for him to choose me again without economic incentives. If we could pull that off, I felt it would put us on a path to the profoundly deep relationship I believed we craved and were capable of.

I was so relieved when he agreed to a separation with the idea we would stay together, bridge our differences, and re-create a more equitable relationship. I was beyond happy that he seemed to understand my need to choose myself AND still be chosen by him. A victory for integrity and a happy ending, all wrapped up in sunsets, rainbows, and fireworks.

No surprise here—it didn't turn out that way. What I saw as an act of union and intimacy for us, he later came to see as rejection. Within days of our separation, he violated our agreements, and he chose to be with another while we were still married.

Sometimes happiness isn't about happy endings. It's about ending something that is a constant source of unhappiness. I don't want to cast blame here or paint myself as a victim. I made choices, too. But in the end, the ultimate choice was to put aside the great compromise and summon the courage to ask for what I need. I hoped I wouldn't have to pay the highest price, but I did.

I chose me, and I'm worth it.

JUSTICE, TRUTH, AND REVELATIONS

After I had evolved beyond the desire to be chosen at all costs, I was overwhelmed with emotion on the day I was once again chosen by a man, this time in a different context. In this instance, the choice wasn't about deeming me worthy as a person, it was about delivering justice. And it happened because I had advocated for myself instead of abandoning myself.

This act turned out to be the key to solving the mystery of why I kept repeating this "choose me" life lesson. Until I was able to correctly identify and name my craving, I could not get the soul-level satisfaction I was after. After so many years, clarity was achieved: I was seeking someone to defend me and to grant me justice.

Sometimes we need to wade into the mess more deeply, feel the pain more keenly, in order to break through to the true nature of the issue. Unless we can get at the root of our choices, we're bound to repeat mistakes and learn lessons over and over. If you have a pattern of dancing with the same difficulty multiple times, it might require profound reflection, sitting a bit longer with the pain until the nuances emerge. That's what happened to me.

In closing my wound, I was determined to be kind to myself as I reviewed my mistakes and the pain they generated. It wouldn't serve to race down the path of "How could I be so dumb?" It wouldn't be useful to dwell on failure and chastisement. Instead, I would sit with the lessons, and the emotions they generated, until I felt a shift. I could congratulate myself for being willing to be with this life lesson as many times as I needed to find integration. When I became willing to just accept it for what it was, I fell through a trapdoor of healing that was profound.

My perspective had been that I kept trying to be chosen in order to heal a pain of feeling unloved. That might have been part of it, sure, but it was so much more. It wasn't just about being desired as a woman. I wanted to be defended as deserving, not only out of love but also out of justice and fairness. And to do that, I had to come out of the shadows of shame, of believing that I should have known better and done things differently. And I had to gather my people—those who would advocate for me when I couldn't do it for myself. To prepare for dissolving my second marriage, I reached out to a team of experts and close friends and bared my soul. When I revealed my bad choices, they jumped in to defend me with a kind of love I hadn't before experienced. Maybe all those years of searching for love was in reality an unrelenting quest for someone to validate that, in some instances, I had been treated unfairly.

In the course of our ongoing divorce proceedings, my lawyer called one day to share the judge's take on the issues at hand. The judge, my lawyer said, had shared his disapproval with my husband's seemingly entitled claims. At the hearing, he ruled in my favor, and I was in shock.

The judge indicated that I wasn't responsible for maintaining my soon-to-be ex-husband's lifestyle or expenses, because he already had benefitted financially far more than his fair share during our short marriage. In multiple hearings, the judge said I shouldn't be responsible for his future nor that of his sons. It felt like a validation that what had been asked of me amounted to the familiar financial (not to mention emotional) extortion that was a big part of my experience of growing up. What I had offered in my leaving, half of what we had, was beyond fair, the judge ruled. In fact, it was generous. I'd believed bribery would be required to keep what was mine, to maintain full ownership of what I had created, and to be in my own life without owing someone else for that privilege. Now I would no longer have to justify why I had the right to enjoy what had always been mine. Vindication resulted in a satisfying revelation. At last, someone chose me, defended me, out of a sense of justice.

The judge hadn't said we both were at fault. He didn't tell me to turn the other cheek or rise above it. He emphatically stated that what had been asked of me was wrong and undeserved. My reaction was tears, and I realized his ruling had satisfied my craving to be chosen, not just for love but as deserving of justice. I wept in relief and happiness at the judge's ruling, which I saw as an affirmation of my self-advocacy. My now ex-husband took the money and ran, straight into the arms of others. I set about the process of healing.

I'd always seen my ability to overfunction as a hard-won badge of honor. I saw needing less and succeeding in spite of my circumstances as strengths. I tolerated semi-abandonment to the point that I abandoned myself. I didn't get what I needed because I didn't allow myself to know I needed it. As I stood up for myself, the judge used his authority to affirm that it wasn't love that would heal me, it was fairness. His decision was the drink that finally slaked my thirst and set a boundary for me that I hadn't been able to set for myself. The ruling got me to a place of refuge where I could hear my own voice again. Liberation.

When the judge chose me, something big fell away. He had given me justice. Now it was time for me to take it from there and be my own champion.

Life is full of challenges, but none is greater than to find your way out of self-abandonment. You have the capacity to heal your wounds, to claim your voice, to acknowledge your worth. You have the right to belong just by being you. You have the right to shatter narratives that keep you stuck or tempt you to play small. Let others help you. Gather a tribe of truth tellers who will advocate for you when you feel you can't. Don't believe the lies people tell you about your own suffering. Look at the reality of what you are currently co-creating and see if that aligns with the life you want to live. You have the power to start your reclamation, to boldly walk yourself to a transformation.

This isn't something I will take for granted, and part of my recovery will be to stay close to the people who can help me see things more clearly—my personal team of upholders. When my gut is reeling and I don't feel I can trust my warped perception, I can go to them. It's okay to ask: "Does this sound right to you? Does this seem fair? Do you see any potential for manipulation or me being taken advantage of?" These people don't collude and reinforce my sense of victimhood—they challenge my thinking and encourage me to advocate for myself. Find people who will help you resist the prisons others try to build around you and establish the clear, bright boundaries that define your liberation.

Your worthiness isn't something you have to earn. You just have to remember it.

And I don't intend to forget that lesson.

BEFORE YOU INVEST IN BEING "THE CHOSEN"

When your state of contentment gets tied to an outcome—securing or maintaining a relationship, snagging a promotion, being allowed membership in a group or clique—it's easy to get lost in the desire to be chosen. Be wary of leaning too far into compromise or conformity, forcing compatibility, and taking your values and needs out of decision-making. It could be a sign you'll eventually topple over.

If the relationship or opportunity feels essential to your happiness, consider this question: Is there something I need to prove, or something in me that I hope might be healed if I am chosen? Does this feel like I'm performing or auditioning rather than being seen for myself and accepted?

A common warning sign is looking to another to give you something you felt robbed of in your past. Trying to heal childhood wounds in adult relationships often leads to self-abandonment, a high price to pay to avoid the work of grieving, healing, and growing.

If your story is, or has been, that being chosen will quash feelings of unworthiness, tell yourself a new story: You are whole and worthy as you are. Who chooses you matters less than the ways you advocate for yourself.

Create guiding questions to measure the ways a friend, love interest, job, boss, or other opportunity will enhance your life above and beyond the satisfaction of being chosen. Here are examples:

Are our lifestyles compatible?

Do the requirements of this job align with the life I hope to live?

Does/will this relationship/job/membership truly improve my life?

What common values do we share? Are there values I might be asked to sacrifice?

How do I feel in their energy?

Does it feel easy to be myself?

Can we feel safe and accepted while challenging and inspiring each other?

Keep your answers grounded in reality. Don't be tempted by how you wish it could be or how it might be if you work hard enough, love big enough, change enough. List the things that you want a partner to do for you and the things that an opportunity might prove about you. Can you skip the middleman and do those things for yourself?

RECOVERING FROM SELF-ABANDONMENT

Sometimes labeling your desires becomes a justification for self-abandonment—they are my soulmate, this is my dream job, this is a once-in-a-lifetime opportunity. If your choice to be chosen begins to feel like you've lost yourself, remember that it's not too late to return to yourself.

Find Self-Compassion

Be kind to yourself. Most regrets are really just decisions and choices made while learning. So, embrace the opportunity for learning. I didn't have two failed marriages, I had two marriages that ended—the only failure would have been not mining the experiences for insight and evolution. I came to understand my relationships with my husbands weren't mistakes. The relationships gave me lessons that were key to my emotional development. With compassion, I could celebrate those lessons and leave the story behind after doing the work of grieving and healing. In my second marriage, I grew to a place where I could thank him while rising up fully to live what I had learned.

Own Your Choices

Nothing changes until you become conscious and aware of patterns that no longer serve you. We are rarely victims of our circumstances, and it is worth the effort to contemplate the why: Why was it important to be chosen? Why were you so taken with the opportunity? What do you think being chosen for this job or as this person's partner will prove or heal in you?

You can't learn in a vacuum. Life's messiness is where lessons are found. You don't go to the gym for a few months and then claim to be forever healthy and fit. Life's learning and healing process will be continuous if you live with curiosity and compassion.

Identify Your Kryptonite

Name and give language to your key learnings. This is juicy work. I had to understand how a woman like me, who had done so well in school and career, who saw herself as strong and capable in my work life, could settle for so little in my home life. I came to see a plausible explanation for the discrepancy between my success at work and my heartbreak in love. At work and at school, I'd had love, support, and mentoring—great teachers, bosses, mentors, peers, and colleagues. What I eventually realized was that in my childhood home, I didn't always get the love, approval, and appreciation I craved from my family. Instead, I learned love was transactional. I had to pay to keep the peace. The craving for that kind of unconditional love, approval, and support was my Kryptonite. I didn't realize I was operating out of that weakness until the end of my second marriage.

Integrate Your Lessons

Understand that when you get swept up in being chosen, you can either let the experience retraumatize you or evolve you. Doing the necessary inner work makes the difference. Dig deep. Are you in some way living the embodiment of childhood wounds? I choose to believe that some people show up to mirror the wounds and my need for healing back to me, messengers who made me sit up and pay attention. Don't abdicate your responsibility to self by painting yourself as a victim. Now that you are paying attention, what will you do differently? How will what you learned aid in your emotional development?

Redefine "Soulmate"

> *A true soul mate is probably the most important person you'll ever meet, because they tear down your walls and smack you awake. But to live with a soul mate forever?*

Nah. Too painful. Soul mates, they come into your life just
to reveal another layer of yourself to you, and then leave.

—ELIZABETH GILBERT, *Eat Pray Love*

I had defined soulmate as a once-in-a-lifetime connection. I was looking for the long shot—the person who could give me a future that would make up for what I lacked from my past. I wanted someone to rescue me from the real work of grieving, healing, growing. I discovered that shortcut doesn't exist.

I redefined soulmate as someone who can be a mirror, the person who shows you what is holding you back, the person who awakens you to how you can change for the better.

Perhaps you need to redefine your label of the opportunity that has spun you off center—is it a dream job? Perhaps a dream job isn't a coveted position in the opinion of others but a position that accommodates the best of you. It provides a container big enough to allow you to grow and fully inhabit your talent. "Once-in-a-lifetime opportunities" are a common story the ego spins to keep you in fear and keep you compromising. The universe is far more generous. A single choice won't make or break you—the margin of error is so much larger!

Maybe the point of life is less about becoming or achieving and more about unbecoming everything that isn't really you. The most meaningful relationship is the one with yourself. Everything else is desire, companionship, and healthy connections. Those won't manifest unless you are at peace.

BEST DATE EVER

It felt like forever since I'd had a really good date. I decided it was time to take the matter into my own hands.

Dating is obviously a big challenge in the time of global pandemic, but I had been feeling a pull. He was someone I had known for a while. I invited him to join me for a long walk on the beach at sunset. Romantic setting, but no pressure. I had only met him face-to-face a few times via Zoom. He was older, smart, funny, and—forgive me for being shallow—handsome. I was attracted to his wisdom and never tired of what he had to say.

"This could be good," I thought.

Instead of primping, I threw on a tank top and beach shorts and slid my feet into flip-flops. I corralled my wild hair, highlighted with silver, back into a ponytail. This was a beach walk, not a gala. No makeup—I was going out in all my natural beauty. My only accessory was a pair of designer sunglasses.

The evening, accentuating its own natural beauty, couldn't

have been more gorgeous. As the sun began its slow descent to the water, the waves in the brilliant blue ocean were occasionally punctured by whales. Sometimes a white misty geyser announced their presence, other times the flirty flash of a fluke waving good-bye. Delightful.

My walking companion was from England, and what is sexier than an accent? His musical, cultured voice was captivating. As the water crashed to shore, the receding foam playfully caressed my feet while I listened to him talk about the pain of the past. At our ages, we'd both had our fair share.

I abruptly stopped the walk, awed as a flock of pelicans, more than I'd ever seen before, flew in formation toward the waves' barrel roll. This spectacle, like the opening scene from a National Geographic special, was worthy of my full presence and attention. The birds broke from formation into a beautiful choreography of graceful soaring and efficient diving. They were like characters in a Disney movie, casting a spell of enchantment, setting the stage in support of a successful date.

I was gobsmacked. This was special, unlike anything I'd seen before. It seemed like a wonderful omen. I had a whimsical thought: Had my date conspired with nature to create an extra good impression? I resumed the conversation, excited to see what else he had to say.

As we strolled, the waves seemed especially flirtatious, as if teasing me to come closer. I let them chase me and then heard a familiar slapping sound. As if on cue, the rays made their frolicsome debut. They always make me laugh. Their exuberant leaps into the air are followed by the flat thwack of their belly flops. No one really knows why they do it—for fun, for protection, as a mating ritual? It seems illogical, even silly. Maybe they do it just to be who they are. Maybe for the joy of it. I think about how I am like them. I leap back into life, dive into the mess, into loving, even when it appears to be illogical. I do it just to be myself, to keep believing in big love and happy endings. I vow to be even more like the rays and to shed the human doubts, the shame, and the constant questioning of choices in a world that demands explanations.

For instance, right now, in this moment, I am doing exactly what feels good on my vulnerable underbelly. Maybe I'll get giggly with David. Here I am, feeling ready to throw myself up and open to new love.

Heading south toward the rocky point, David's voice was hypnotic, and suddenly the conversation got deep. He started telling me about the time he'd been preparing for a retreat with a group of nuns. He felt unworthy to lead their work, and apparently it showed. Eventually, he was called out by a nun who could see his hesitancy to step with faith into the future. He had shared with them, and now recounted to me, one of his own deepest wounds. Such an open-hearted and vulnerable man! I felt seen as he affirmed that we shared the same core wounds. In that moment with the nuns, he told me, his tears flowed without the usual accompanying shame. Tears of relief and healing. The experience had been a breakthrough for him, returning him to the path of love.

David asked me to consider an intriguing question: What is *your* greatest wound? What are the wounds you fear opening up again, the ones from which you protect yourself? The ones that might rob you of new love?

Wow, I think. On one hand, this is the kind of intimate conversation I've longed for with a man, but . . . do I really want to go there?

Then again, reflecting on the past to transform the present has led to some of the most enriching conversations I've ever had. I immersed myself in memories and pondered the question as the seductive sun moved closer to the water, eager for its own good-night kiss.

He suggested I think about the first time I felt heartbroken, rejected, or betrayed by someone who should have cared for me. Consider how it might change, he suggested, if you were willing to fully experience it. Don't just remember it. Experience it deeply, wholly. Claim it as yours. Maybe that would transmute the event into something new.

With a deep breath, I jumped into the abyss of my hard memories, looking for wounds to open and possibly heal.

I thought about the fury of my older sisters who were obliged to take care of me when they were young and needy, too. I listened to the waves' percussion as they pounded the shore and felt something that had been unyielding begin to loosen. Long-held, rock-hard resentments were being worn away.

As my heart began to open, other wounds surfaced. I thought about the failed promises of my two marriages. The horrifying discovery of my first husband's infidelities after I had saved his life after an accident and stood by him during a long, difficult recovery. I recalled the betrayal from my second marriage. My husband and I had been struggling with complex issues for years. In the fall, we agreed to separate but remain faithful to one another, confident that we would figure it out. Then I found out he was sleeping with his high school sweetheart. His stepmom even shared the news that he wanted to bring her to a family Christmas celebration. Determined not to let betrayal ruin us, I forgave him. We reconciled. Then I confronted the hard reality that his desire to reconcile didn't come with a willingness to do the hard work of healing and building a different future. He refused to fully commit. Betrayal upon betrayal—twice rejected by the same love. It felt like the ultimate cruelty.

Oh, the pain of that! As I stared at nature's display, focusing on David's gentle voice, my pain began to transmute, giving me my own breakthrough. I had loved my husbands, and yet they were never really mine. I didn't own them. They weren't my property. How could they betray me? Their crime, in my eyes, was their choice to withhold something I wanted, a future I'd hoped for. Their preference was for someone or something else. If I really loved them and wanted them to be happy, I could make peace with the fact that they found greater happiness in their lives with others. Love cannot be a demand. They were with me until they weren't. Some of the old, familiar pain began to ease, the beginnings of liberation.

Finally, one of my deepest wounds called for attention. It happened in high school, during the throes of my parents' difficult divorce, which I remember as one of the worst periods of my life.

I still remember the excitement I felt hearing my name over the school's loudspeaker. I had been nominated as homecoming royalty. I hadn't dared to dream of being that popular. I had staked my identity on being helpful and smart, which allowed me the occasion to hang out with the popular. Then again, I hung out with everyone, refusing to join cliques, being equally friendly with the underdogs, the rebellious, and the bright. I made a point of sitting at lunch with those who had been shunned. I volunteered to help anyone who struggled. I was nice. I forgave. I believed in second chances. And now the payoff—homecoming royalty!

When everyone in my homeroom started laughing, I was confused. Another announcement came over the loudspeaker. Would the male candidate and I please report to the superintendent's office? The young man, who was seen as one of the weirdest kids in my class, also had been elected to the homecoming court. He struggled in school and barely spoke. He was known for meowing at people to keep them away from his locker.

After we arrived at the office, the superintendent told us that our classmates had engineered our nominations as a cruel practical joke. He apologized and told us they would be dealt with. He suggested we both decline the nominations. My fellow nominee, withering with embarrassment in this savage spotlight, immediately said yes, clearly relieved to escape.

I felt lost, frozen by betrayal and humiliation. My reality had just been shattered. I thought these people were my friends, and now I didn't know where I stood. I had been so nice to everyone! It felt like a strange rendition of that horror movie *Carrie*. I told the superintendent I wanted to think about it overnight.

My mom encouraged me to shake off the pain and to enjoy homecoming. She argued my class had just wanted to have a little fun with me, and I could ride in the parade with the replacement candidate, a really great guy. Reluctantly, I signed up for the high road—the hardest road—riding in the parade while knowing I wasn't who they really wanted, that I wasn't deserving of the honor. I hated that the parade was a façade, but I kept it together, publicly smiling and waving.

Every time someone in my life made a choice that felt like a betrayal or rejection, the gut-crushing feeling of that homecoming debacle would revisit me.

I returned to David's questions: Could I see this for what it was? Could I experience it fully and feel the shifts? His questions and my deep reflections led me to a release I didn't expect. I realized that these painful experiences, which left me feeling rejected and betrayed, had little to do with me. What had happened was a sick joke by a bunch of teenagers who were also struggling to figure themselves out. What they did was about their demons, not mine. In that moment, the hurt fell away. What I had believed all these years wasn't even true. The relief I felt in that moment was like a deep exhale after a long-held breath.

I fixed my gaze on the clouds, painted by the sun in an array of colors as if to affirm and support my moment of healing. I turned to the east and watched the moon rising over the mauve mountains bathed in evening shadows.

It was quiet, and yet nature, acting as the perfect matchmaker, conducted a sweet, romantic score with the waves' soothing songs. It was as if she was pulling out all the stops, creating glorious displays for my benefit and whispering, "I am here for you. I'll do my part to make this an awesome date." With David's seductive voice continuing in my ear, I headed home.

I could scarcely believe my good fortune. What a walk! Nature was putting on a command performance. My companion's deep questions had sparked deep contemplation that led me to a sort of wholeness I have rarely felt in my life. This shift in perspective felt miraculous. And I didn't even have to dress up for it!

But one more surprise awaited. As I approached my house, I heard bells ringing. The colorful cows of the Baja were walking leisurely toward me, the calves stumbling along near their mamas. It's not unusual to see a few random cows walking the beach, but this was a large herd, ambling along in a line of twos and threes. More than twenty, I estimated, in every imaginable cow color. I heard and felt the vibrations of their lowing. A few of them dipped their horns at me as they walked past, as if in deep reverence for who I am and what I had experienced.

I burst out laughing. My homecoming parade! This time, it was fully deserved and fully enjoyed. I pulled out my phone. This moment of joy and healing needed to be captured on video.

The sun was about to give the water its long-awaited nightly kiss, and the sky was a brilliant benediction. I turned off David Whyte's podcast. We would meet again tomorrow. I climbed the stairs, poured myself a glass of wine, and sat on the balcony to wait for the last ray of the sun to wink out—the green flash. It didn't disappoint.

I felt utterly content and satisfied. In the most unexpected way, I had found, in myself, new love and ever-present companionship.

Best date ever.

SUNDAY-MORNING SERVICE IN THE DESERT

On a Sunday morning in late February, I am attending the church of the cacti in the Mexican Baja. I am flanked by mountains, and although I can't see it, the Pacific Ocean crashes to shore behind me, creating a sacred sanctuary for meditative self-reflection and the setting of big intentions.

I have been dipped in joy. The sun washes over the mountains and crowns the cactus with bright yellow haloes. I walk the gravel road in front of my new home with outstretched arms, open-hearted. I breathe in this place of peace, and I breathe out the gratitude I feel for having landed here. I stretch my arms wider, chest high, my face to the sky, not caring what anyone might think. I am listening closely to what my body craves and fulfilling the craving.

For months, I had felt as if I were living in the belly of Jonah's whale, only to find myself coughed up in this magical place where I have restored my soul. The mountains are my guardians, the cacti are my colleagues, the prickly pear plants and I worship the sun. Here is evidence that the universe loves me. What a happy accident to have ended up here. Except, really, I don't believe it was an accident.

Just over a year ago I was in this same place, my stomach knotted, my soul exhausted, and my heart breaking as I contemplated losing a big love and the Baja house of our dreams. A few months later, I got stranded here, facing the loss of my business, mourning the sudden loss of my fourteen-year-old nephew, worried about a tricky health diagnosis, accompanying my dearest friend to her imminent death, all while negotiating an unwanted and painful divorce. I was also trying to figure out how the hell I was going to get this book done. Mess upon mess upon mess.

And here I was, today, on this glorious Sunday morning, communing with the cacti with a heart bursting with gratitude, having rediscovered that the price of not knowing yourself is high, and the price of not living true to yourself is even higher.

How can I be so giddy, so happy in the aftermath of a supreme shitshow of a year, I ask myself. But I know the answer: Happiness isn't about what is happening in your external life. It's about how you cultivate your internal life.

My life fell apart, and as I let go, my new life fell into place. In falling apart, I fell through some sort of mystical trapdoor. Every loss, every letting go, opened me up to something amazing.

I lost the person I had called the love of my life and found greater loves in my life: dear new friends, a stunningly beautiful place to live, a caring community to be part of, and a deeper, truer love of myself. And the whales, those glorious, majestic whales.

As millions of dollars in contracts disappeared in 2020, I thought I had lost my business. And then I realized I had found my business. My business is helping others, and I discovered creative new ways to do that in a way that preserves the peace in my life.

I got stranded, which was rescue in disguise. If someone had said to me, "Cy, what you need is to take three months off, enter into deep solitude and self-care, and to be there for your best friend as she's dying," I never would have allowed myself the luxury of such a retreat. But the world health crisis put me into a forced time out, reality drowning out the sound of my own voice saying, "I would love to, but I can't."

Surrendering to life in lockdown allowed me to open up completely. I chose to be a monk, not a prisoner. The solitude opened my eyes, my heart, my creativity. My small dreams for the future and the world suddenly enlarged.

I came for a visit and accidentally found my new place in the world. I had been following a star that I didn't even realize was there. It had hidden behind the stormy clouds, and when the clouds parted, it suddenly revealed its brilliance. My intuition was way ahead of me, setting me up for what I needed before I knew I would need it. I call that the "invisible help." Trust it to provide what you need when you need it.

My life came undone, and I sat among the shards of loss and heartbreak as what was not meant for me fell away, the only thing remaining was what I needed.

I got a book contract to write about how you should live, and instead I wrote a book about how I have lived.

My mind is blown by how the universe moved when I surrendered and got out of the way. What a different place I'm in after one year. The mess? You and I know the mess well. It's where the perfect you meets the imperfect world. It is what I call reality—that messy place where you bring your hard-earned wisdom out into the world and love big. The mess is where grace and gratitude meet loss and pain to find joy and resurrection.

You CAN be happy in the mess, because happiness is not an emotion or a feeling—those are too dependent on external circumstances. You don't have to defer happiness until you get the perfect job, find the perfect partner, build your dream house. It's not necessary for all the stars to align. Happiness is the consistent hum of contentment, ever present, just waiting for you to get quiet enough to hear it. Happiness is knowing that all is well, all will be well. It will all turn out in the end, or it's not the end.

Happiness is the sturdy container large enough to hold the contradictions, the confusion, the vulnerability until you once again find the love.

"Happiness is an inside job" is a cliché because it's a fundamental truth. Look to the future with no expectation and with great expectancy. If you can be with whatever is happening, knowing that it's supposed to be happening, you'll find comfort. When you develop a deep sense of knowing that the universe has your back, you can be consistently content. When you commit to a love affair with life, including its messiness and heartbreak, happiness is inevitable. You are the cowriter of your own great life story.

No happiness factory exists. Happiness can't be manufactured, and it doesn't come from achievement or acquisition. Your natural state is waiting to be revealed in the now by going within, getting clear about who you are, then letting everything that isn't supportive or fulfilling fall away. Fulfillment is different than pleasure. Pleasure and pain are a duality, and both fade away with time. Happiness and contentment transcend pleasure and pain.

Find *your* place, a space that feels safe and promotes contemplation, self-reflection. Find a place where you can grieve, and heal, and grow. For me, it's mostly been at the water's edge.

Be wary of what you think you know for sure. Your first reactions often spring from the ego's story. I've discovered when I question the ego's story, which is typically a story of hurt or harm, I can find an opposite and greater truth if I allow it.

In my year of super messy living, I sustained happiness by adhering to my habits, dedications, and surrender: meditation, walks in nature, deep reflection, contemplation, making amends, forgiving others, letting go, and evolving—otherwise, I don't know how I would have survived.

YOURS FOR THE ASKING

In the Sunday worship of my youth, right before communion, we'd be called to the metaphorical practice of ingesting a wafer that signified Christ. The priest issued a call, an invitation to transcend, and the response was "Only say the word, and I shall be healed."

I love those words because they help me remember that's all it really takes. You are never far from source. Indeed, you are never separate from source. Miracles happen daily, and they can come in the form of little shifts in perception.

This year, possibly the messiest in my life so far, I have found myself right where I belong. I committed to creating a life at the water so I can leave behind the life that made me retreat to the water. At the water, I am reflected, baptized, soothed, washed clean.

Do I sometimes yearn for something different than what I have? Sadly, too often. Do I perfectly practice what I preach? Sadly, not often enough. Do I pine for the past? Almost daily. I know I can never stop doing the work.

One truth I know for sure: there are many ways to go backward, but only one way forward, and that's with lots of love.

Your work, should you choose to accept it, is to stop forgetting. Any time you lose your bliss, your contentment, your happiness, look up from the mess and re-remember who you really are. When in doubt, try loosening fear with love. It never fails. You can't find a way to bring the love into the moment or the situation? No worries, that is excellent data on where you need to evolve next. Lovevolve, lovevolve, lovevolve—that is the happiness cycle. That is the shift in perspective that calls in the miracles.

Find your people and love them big.

Use love and your hard-earned inner wisdom to wade fearlessly into the beautiful mess.

Help wherever and whenever you can.

Walk with grace, gratitude, and an open heart and mind.

Practice the habits and dedications that will let you walk peacefully in the world.

Evolve yourself.

Do this until the teacher calls savasana, and you will have lived a happy life.

Love wins. Love always wins. I promise.

ACKNOWLEDGMENTS

A major source of my contentment is that I am so well loved and supported by brilliant, courageous, and wise humans on the daily, people who believe in me and in my work. For that I am so very grateful and humbled.

Giles Anderson—you are a fantastic agent and a wise and supportive thought partner. I am a published author because of you. I am so grateful that you called me that day on the beach and posed the question: "Have you ever considered writing a book?" You made hope a possibility and helped me bring four beautiful books into the world. Every time I see one of our book covers, I smile.

George Witte and the team at St. Martin's Press—thank you, for believing in the power of my work and the necessity of this personal story in the midst of world upheaval. The finishing touches you add to my work are always spectacular. This is a good book.

Maren Showkeir—dearest friend and like-minded editor extraordinaire! I will always treasure our days and nights in the magical Baja, writing, dancing, and sharing heart-to-heart. I love that you find the perfect language to share what is in my heart and the exact names for the wisdom we all need to remember. Your sweet, gentle kindness was exactly the flavor of love I needed to tell my most personal stories. You are a talented midwife, birthing beautiful books into the world.

Pam Bourne, Virginia Albers, and Audrey Svane—brave, fierce, warriors of justice who fought for me when I was too heartbroken and disillusioned to fight for myself. Having women like you on my side healed something deep in me, changing how I walk in this world. Never again will I doubt my worth and/or be willing to be emotionally extorted by others.

Terry, Mike, and Lorann—thank you, for entering into the difficult work of saving a sister. You were all so willing to give what you could. I loved our time together, even though the circumstances weren't lovely at all.

Andrea, Ana, Maren, and Pam—my loyal, loving, girlfriends. Together we made it through a beautiful, tragic year and emerged soul sisters. I simply adore the four of you.

Jackie, my wise, feminist counsel. You helped me see reality and supported me as I left behind a world no longer meant for me. Even more importantly, you were my shepherd in the "in between" times—that year between losing a life I loved and building a life I would love next. I am loving what I am building.

Linda and Melanie—my welcoming committee to Mexico, now dearest friends. Thank you, for walking me day after day through the church of the cacti, trusting that our steps together could help heal my heart and get me dreaming again. I am home now.

Jason, my Baja angel—the space you are building to hold all my new dreams is beautiful and healing. Your support in my times of need were crucial in building my confidence that I could create a new life *"en la playa."*

Elisa, my sweet niece, you have been an inspiration to me as I have watched you find a way to live with the heartbreak of losing our sweet, smiling Drew and keep your kind heart open and caring about me. Thanks, for letting me use your story to help others find a way through the pain.

The Reality-Based Leadership Dream Team: George, Alex, Sara, Maria, and Ana!!!! Without you, Operation Free Cy 2020 would not have been possible. Your loyalty and the incredible effort you put into defending, recovering, investigating, rebuilding, supporting, and cleaning up the remnants, all while surviving the year that was COVID, are mind-boggling. I couldn't imagine what life could be with every part of our business cleaned up, simplified, and running effortlessly. But you could, and you created that reality. We are back to living the drama-free work life that we know is possible.

The most enduring love and my life force comes from my four amazing sons. George, Charles, Henry, and William, I am so blessed to have you in my life. Your love is a superpower, fixing what is broken, soothing my hurts, healing my heartbreaks, forgiving my transgressions, and believing in my dreams. (Also, moving my boxes.) Every day, I am touched by your unconditional love and support.

My lakeside roommates, the Dorrs, provided the soft place to land that I had been craving for years. You were there to hold the center—personally and professionally—as I realized the only life I could save was my own. Thank you, for holding space and loving me all the while. And thanks for your best work yet: Archie. Onward to building an amazing legacy together.

ArchieMan! You, my sweet soul, have been the ultimate blessing

ACKNOWLEDGMENTS

to me. Your presence in my life is a constant reminder that there are many ways backward but only one way forward—love.

To my fans—the original Life's Messy, Live Happy group—you are living proof of our ability to live happy in a messy world.

Always know one thing for sure. #LoveWins.